Lea Maria Flinkman 04/18/1950-12/25/2019

To the most courageous, loving woman Lea, who dedicated her life to be able to channel this book.

To Lea, may her memory live forever.

Note from the translator.

This publication is a translation from Finnish to English from my beloved, Lea Flinkman's journals.

In 1980 she developed a gift for automatic writings.

She began with communicating with the spirit world, at times negative energy would come through and as she continued to write she progressed to communicate with humanoids called Men, Sons of Gods.

These writings later as Sons of God referred to as telepathy, not automatic writings. In the early 1990's she also began to channel the three humanoids, Sons of God, the two whose names I knew were Adam and Cirius. When this channeling occurred, the energy level changed dramatically, this energy is so powerful, an experience of Heaven would be the only way to describe it. Men also knew every detail of our lives and gave us spiritual teaching. These encounters lasted for a few years.

All the way to the end of her life, every morning (or after a nap) she described speaking with someone, yet not able to remember the contents of the conversations. She also had multiple visions of Men and she had three near death experiences, where she always saw bright light, experienced unconditional love and saw the three Men wearing gray overalls. In each near-death experience, she was asked if she wanted to go with them or return to life, she chose life in each one.

She was also a very gifted psychic and a medium, often seeing ghosts, she had many visions of the future that later came true. She had many paranormal and extraterrestrial experiences, both positive and negative.

I will go into more detail about her encounters when I publish her biography. She was a writer, a poet and a painter, a strong independent intelligent woman.

The Path of the Four Fires

Lea M Flinkman

Copyright 2022 all rights reserved.

No part of this publication may be reproduced, distributed, or transmitted or changed in any form in any means, including photocopying, recording or other electronic or mechanical methods, without permission from the publisher, except as permitted by U.S copyright law.

To the maximum extent permitted by law, the translators and publishers of this book are not liable for the contents of this book.

This book was written as it was channeled and by law not one word can be altered, added, or subtracted from its original version.

ISBNs: (979-8-9877720-0-3 soft cover), (979-89877720-2-7 hard cover)

www.thepathofthefourfires.com

This book is also available in Finnish language as it was originally written in Finnish language.

It has been my greatest honor and gift to have shared my life with Lea, as my teacher, my best friend and my mother, my greatest love.

This book is her life's work, and as my greatest honor I had the opportunity to be a part of it.

M.D

Note from the editor:

    The following text is something that I cannot entirely explain. As you may have read from the translator's note, this information was directly channeled through my grandmother in the form of an automatic writing from a collective of beings known simply as, "The Sons of God" These beings are also known to take the name of "The Storks" The original form of the text is in the Finnish language and as such the translation may appear to be unconforming to traditional ideas of English sentence structure and order in general. Additionally, the original source material is quite literally a complex poem that when translated does not accurately represent the exact form from which the text was conveyed. This however should not dissuade the reader as the information present holds great wisdom and your understanding of it will still hold true.

J.T.

"There is only one path, one truth"

Men/Sons of God

THE PATH OF THE FOUR FIRES

Children of the Earth, you are Children of the Earth.

Why are you Children of the Earth?

Fighting between the spirit and the Earth, Children of the Earth.

The Earth takes what belongs to the Earth and the spirit will go where it belongs.

The Earth was born of pain and death, do not be ashamed that you are Children of the Earth.

The Earth is hard and cruel, that is why you are here.

This is no longer a paradise.

Life is hard, cruel and raw for the Children of the Earth,

if you are on Earth, you are a Child of Earth.

Learn, you are here to learn.

Everything has its reason. When the time comes, be ready to be responsible for your actions.

From the Earth you pay the Earth.

From the spirit you pay to God,

and then there is Satan.

We did not come here to judge.

You judge yourselves.

We are not angels, angel is only a word.

We can only explain through words, and the words will be distorted.

How do you compare souls? With words and wrong again,

you feel a lot of pain and each one of you is searching for the light.

We can say we are the descendants of God, but what difference does it make anymore.

Come home if you want.

If you are on Earth, you are Children of the Earth.

Do not cry, you are here to learn.

Sometimes what we say vanishes into your pain.

Rise above your pain.

With what to rise?

If you have hope, it is taken away.

If you have light, it will be dimmed.

If you have wings, they are cut off.

We do listen to you, and we answer, but you cannot hear us.

The light is, but you cannot find it.

There is a voice, but you do not hear it.

You have to come to us, because we also come to you.

The path on Earth has never been easy but there is a path.

Learn how to love right, learn how to recognize God's Divine Love.

The Earth gives you a face and it grows.

God gave you a spirit and it remains and because you have a path, then walk it.

You do not have a teacher, but yet the teacher is.

We do not judge, we love.

Sons of God/Men from direct verbal contact, channeled through Lea.

(As follows are a series of answers to questions not explicitly stated within the original source material.)

Because this is also a battle about who wins, the evil wants its part in the information that you will bring to people. You will learn to produce telepathy that will mainly be from Men and no longer from anywhere else. Once you have developed in this matter well enough you can begin the work you are here for. Men will come if you invite us and if you want, we can come today, (in reference to a direct contact) although we can remain in contact like this as well.

Lea, if you want us to put this telepathy try not to think. If you cannot control your thoughts, we cannot explain anything. Why can't we do this with your daughters? We cannot because they do not know how to control their minds, they want to, but they cannot. Others who have been here have been here to help. Let us know what you would like to know. We are pushing for you not to accept others, take Men and do not take others. Do not take spirits. Men do not conduct horrible experiments or take people into our ships. The movie that you saw, (Fire in the Sky) they are evil. Men cannot hide the experiments of the evil ones or prevent their telepathy. They produce the type of telepathy wherein people become evil. We do not threaten, and if we send dreams, these dreams are not evil.

We do not always send telepathy or do direct contact. Some contacts are not from us and surprisingly you realize that these connections work in the same pattern as your automatic writings. When you learn to control this, you will know when Men come or when something else might come. When we want to establish contact you can feel it, we will send telepathy telling you that we are beginning contact. As we begin you also become very spiritual and happy.

When you are in a bad mood we cannot come, others can and what is worse is that the evil spirit who is always near can come through.

Women want men because they want to eliminate their problems. They think that a man can help them. Men think the same way, they run away from their problems to a woman. No matter what, the problems will remain.

We are Sons of the Heaven, we are not spirits like you are thinking right now. We are not dead like spirits. They also know how to do this, but not in the same way we do. (In reference to the automatic writings.) They make an announcement that they are coming through. First, they harass you for a while like the evil spirit that always tries to come through. It produced a lot of text, although you did not receive what it said. At the moment we are quite close to Earth, we want to be in contact. Due to the distance our contact will not be so short compared to when we go further away. We cannot help time and no matter what happens to you try not to care. You will understand later. We are here now and although you are very intelligent, you cannot understand everything.

We have been here for a very long time, way before you were born, and we are still here. We are rather old, and in a way very different. We live for a long time. We live to be much older than humans and we can choose when we are born again. There is no karma that can hold us, we are free to live as we choose. We do not think that death is a difficult thought. When we die, we come back together with the ones we choose. We never insult or hurt one another; we live in complete peace. But we cannot, nor do we want to explain time, it happens when the time comes. In telepathy we do so that those who are in telepathy will receive thoughts from the second level where we are. We are not going to explain this any better.

Lea although this is only telepathy, we are here only because soon you will begin your work, a telepathy work, overall, it is rather fun after all. Lea we have an idea, we can be here and put telepathy, what have you thought about all this? Men will only begin telepathy provided that you would like us to. We say that time exists but overcome it, time is on our side, nice things are on our side, provided that you had been in a happy marriage previously, then you would be in a difficult one now, but because the evil time is behind you, you can now wait for the good times.

Everyone has to pay for their karma, that cannot be prevented, after the karma has been paid things can ease up a little bit, we can further explain. Although you are not very happy at the moment and you don't want anyone in your life, soon that will be true that you are together with someone and happy when you are no longer alone, but only so that you wouldn't spend so much time here, you spend too much time in telepathy. Lea if you cannot be without these (automatic writings) then let us know. There are many spirits in the lower level that want to come through, if you are not in the correct vibrational level, the spirits might come, provided that you don't understand or you receive unclear information, the spirits may have caused that.

You have understood correctly, and many things have been revealed. It is also bad that the evil spirit was here on Earth when Jesus was here and the evil spirit will always be here on Earth because this Earth is a place where people are tempted. They are allowed to be here and they never have peace. It is true, it will be tied, and its power will be taken away. It is a kind of a space where it can exist (probably about the evil spirits) if not Satan. It coincides with the time that it is prepared for Satan. Doing evil does not help ever. An evildoer always has to continue to do evil so that they are able to rest if even for a moment. We do not want to explain everything in telepathy, you can understand on your own. We can physically be on Earth, although we can also use the phone.

There is real love like Lea's love but is it Lea's? This is not a way one can get love. How can one get love? Maybe there is no love unless it exists in the heart of a human. Love is what the human is. Each one loves in accordance with their own ability. That is that. Then who loves who? That is another story, it is always a secret. Who loves who and why? Here we love differently. First of all, we do not love as you do. Men take such a wife who is suitable, one who is on the same vibrational level. Usually this type of union lasts. Men here do not have other relationships. We do not want to wound our wives and our wives do not want to wound their husbands. Usually because we wait for someone who is right for us to come when it is time. Sometimes if the spouses do not want to live together, it is because they want to live alone. It sounds rather funny but sometimes humans fall in love too much and they lose their minds. That can often be a reason why some want to live alone. You should not play with emotions.

We are protected from evil because of the way we live, although evil can cause negative vibrations. We are now ready to stop, like you are. If you want more information, be in contact.

Lea, do not care if the telepathy is unclear in this way, or if others can get through. At times, the telepathy can have incorrect information. There is a troublesome spirit here again who is seeking for a connection. He is just an ordinary man who died in a car accident and would like to get more time.

This way we can also present things later if necessary. We do not have any secrets in God's Kingdom. We can speak to another who is waiting, and we can also use the Bible as an aide in this. If you want, we can talk about the Bible if it helps people better understand this, we only want to know if you agree. Not everything is always correct because we do not always understand what you ask. Sometimes there are mistakes. We sing when it is our time to sing.

We are here and we are helping you learn what everything is about. We will not put this in unless you want to. We are here to help mankind so that they can learn to live right. We will not help unless it is what you want. We cannot stop evil, and neither can anyone, unless they themselves accept the evil, that is the truth, we do not accept evil. We cannot help with material things. We help with spiritual development. We cannot change the turn of events, we cannot even if we wanted to. Life is often quite strenuous between work and so on, and then still all the relationships. We cannot change that. Days are rather bad day behind many closed eyes. We cannot change people and if we could, we would not be here. It is clear that humans have not learned one important lesson, do not do evil, not even to your worst enemy. It is an important lesson. Do not take revenge, do not do evil and the pain will end.

Lea, there was a lot of evil energy here and we received evil energy. There is no playing with fire, that fire was love that does not burn for long, true love can handle a lot. There was a lot of evil energy, and it came here. We put it away. We will not put anything evil in this. If evil comes here, it comes from Satan by hating in that way. Write this and send the evil energy back to the evil psychic who is sending it.

When you begin this, you should not care about the evil psychic, do not care about what he has done. If you do care, then he can get a hold on you. Humanoids choose. Forgive, provided that you cannot remove the evil, the humanoids bring it back because the evil does not want for you to achieve this contact, provided that couldn't remove that evil then another evil would come. Don't fight it when it doesn't want or let it be when it doesn't want to leave. What makes it serious is when you do not want to remove it. When the evil is gone, the work is finished. When you have finished this work, the evil will go away on its own.

We come if you want, the Storks trust that you will choose what to explain. They want you to learn what you want to explain, that you do not think that everything you think about is what Men explain. That spell has been here from the beginning. That although you want to be yourself, you cannot live unless you remain in contact with the evil psychic. This is the reason we want you to be free from all ties. Humanoids take care of the spirit. We brought life from the spirit world and when Satan created a world where he can do what he wants he could not however come to that world where evil things do not belong.

Men want you to send it and choose the body that sends the book forward. We want it to be under your name so that the promise you once gave will be wiped away. Humanoids want you to put your own union on fire because of this.

You do not understand the acts of the body, of which there are many. We come here, Men come here, we do not place this onto anyone else. Many think they can trust in this way.

If you have not been purified, we do not come. We don't do this. We do not search. We do not need this. Men do not want to explain more than what we have in direct contact.

All people, even young people become disappointed in love. Nobody has the strength to believe in love anymore. When the time comes where everyone is sick, they will believe that it is the time in which telepathy comes from Heaven. They will learn that it is not self-evident with whom to sleep with, they will learn from love. At the moment people still believe that sex is love, and that it is without a doubt the love of Satan.

We cannot prevent what will happen or what has already happened. The evil has always been and always will be. Men come here, although you were able to receive Men yesterday, you were not happy as we begun. When we begin direct contact, we want you to be happy and for you to wish to be in contact with us. Today you felt anxious, and you still do. You do not know what to do. Maybe pray a little. Maybe begin to pray when taking contact with Men. When you realize what happens between Heaven and Earth. As you rest and think about what has happened to you when the low spirit came, you were given memories that were not true. You were given secret explanations that you could not understand and when you continued the evil spirits came and began the work that at that moment you tried to stop. The evil spirits came and momentarily took over your body. During that time you received evil telepathy and states of anguish and pain. Why do you doubt that? Provided that I am the only one who could be here.

We cannot come if you are in bad telepathy, if you were not then everything would be good.

When now our loved Lea you realize and you make contact with us again you will know that although there is a lot of evil here, there is something perfect here, and what is perfect are the humanoids. We are not evil, nor do we want to produce any evil. Humanoids do not want to explain. The Storks bring thoughts.

When men ridicule you, you will realize that you are not as they wish you to be. This is only because you are different, and the men whom you meet cannot love you when you do not think like women on Earth, nor live like humans. They do not know how to love you.

Humanoids are not claiming that there would not always be someone who knows how to love. When you finally realize that the one you love is not as you wish them to be, you can no longer love them. Provided that you want to, you can go out and meet someone and have a little fun, but you cannot love him, although you can have a little fun.

Provided that we come and explain what is going on, we are not saying that everything is ok, many things are wrong. When you realize why you have anxiety today, then you realize what is the truth. Some support and some ridicule, what is the truth? If you want, you can soon understand what that is about.

We will not put this in unless you want to, we will if you want. Although you want to trust, you cannot. You doubt and you doubt. This means that you have begun this work that is in telepathy. Humanoids cannot trust Lea if you do not care about what the work that you do is. Lea, if you do not care, someone else can do it, but can they? What is Lea's work? Lea, please understand it is important that this work is done on a healthy basis. Men were coming, the Storks wanted to come. Lea, we want you to finish this work, there is nothing else, just continue doing this work. On the mountains (Verte) there was a low spirit, it touched Lea and gave Lea evil telepathy. Humanoids will now begin a new exiting program.

THE PATH OF THE FOUR FIRES

We are The Sons of Heaven, we are space humans, we are humanoids, we are not dead, and we are not ghosts.

When you came into this life, we were with you, when you were growing up, we were with you, and when you were an adult, we were with you. Throughout your living life, we were in contact with you. There were many genetic mistakes, and you did not know how to be as you were meant to be. We could not prevent the evil things that happened, some of it was karma. You also inherited bad genes from your mother's side that made you too sensitive. As you know you were quite depressed from time to time, nothing could take away your pain. We made it so that you could be more in contact with us. We were trying to make it easier for you to adapt to a human's life, but you could not adjust. You had lived through many reincarnations, and were old spiritually, but you could not become conditioned to the human way of life or their thought processes. That is why so often you became our key from heaven.

We had thought to have you marry a very nice young man. Instead, you decided to leave with the one you later married. This was a bad mistake because he was evil, but it was also your karma. You were the chosen one and you chose him. Once you realized what he was, it was too late and you could not escape him. Nobody cared about what happened to you or your children because of him. He was one of Satan's men. His mother was evil as well. Although she was religious, she had let evil in. A grave is waiting for her. She could have been different than who she was.

There were many things that you had never wished for in your life, but now all that has happened is over. The thoughts that you had, that there is nothing you did not feel, or nothing you did not experience, is true. So, if you are tired and burned out, at least you are alive and can regain your balance. We cannot say that you got the easy way out, you just had to live a little too much during one lifetime. Nobody could have lived through all that you did and kept their sanity, but you did because you are not a Child of Earth. Your consciousness is in a much higher level, and spiritually you are much higher. Lea was able to do all that because her consciousness was much higher and spiritually, she was in much higher plane. Other people were always against her because she was always right. Provide that she had had a good life she would have been able to go very far in life, but all this had to happen. Alone she had to face evil people, betrayals, and wickedness, she helped many without ever receiving any help for herself. Provided that you think she was not one of us, then you yourself are nothing but a Child of Satan. Through Lea we will put all the things we want to explain. She never cared for fame and fortune, if she had she would have received it, but she didn't want anything that wasn't real for her, she knew that whatever she was given was what belong to her. We are not claiming that she was one who would have stood in the crowd when horrible things happened, she didn't care what happened when someone's time had to be taken away. She just not one of those people who would have enjoyed other's problems. Now her time has come full. All of her suffering history has been closed to Men's burial chambers, we have each of her previous Men's Four Laws. Men meaning Men who will come after she has to leave.

We are Men. We are Sons of God, we are here at the top of the sky, and we want to leave this message to our brothers, the Children of the Earth.

We will begin by explaining who Lea is.

Lea lived in Finland and she is one of us. She has been under our testing her entire life. We have been testing to see whether she would be right for this work. Not only did she have to overcome her own problems, but she also had to overcome the testing we put her through.

Now she is ready, she had to do all of this work alone because she needed to be strong. Many received help and found a companion, but she had to give up everything, even her own daughters. She was willing to give up the last person who loved her so that she could live in truth. She always chose the truth no matter what. In this way, she was also always searching for the truth. She was offered many lies yet she always chose the truth. We do not want anyone to think that what we say is not what we mean.

We are The Sons of the Heaven; we are here on top of the sky. We will leave this message to our brothers, the Children of the Earth.

Men, Sons of God, begin.

Children of the Earth who live in grief and pain, you have a lot to learn. Everyone who we have sent to help you were betrayed, abandoned, and even worse, ridiculed by you. Why do we even want to help you when we do not owe you anything? We do not have to teach you, but we come back again and again, and we try to help you so that you can realize that what has always been given to you will also be taken away from you.

You have been given life, and you have been given yet another opportunity to learn. Every time you are given life, you are given another chance. Why don't you understand that a state called purgatory exists within you? When you are not in harmony with the Laws of God and with yourselves, you will go into a state of purgatory. When you are in this state of purgatory, you want all that you have been given to be taken away and put in a coffin so that you can have peace. Why do you want to die when you have all the opportunities to become happy and make other people around you happy as well?

As you know, life is not what you want it to be, life exists under its own laws. When you die, you cannot take anything with you. Everything that you had will stay here. What do you think will follow you? Your thoughts, your actions and everything that you have been. Maybe when it is all over, you will realize that you were just an empty bag that no one will miss. Why not help your neighbor and why not learn how to love right so that what you take with you would be something you want to keep?

Life is not easy, not even for those whose life is in order. Why do you envy each other when nobody's life is easy? If you want to know, we can explain to you what life is all about. If you want to know, we can explain to you what death is all about. If you really want to know, we can tell you who is one of your own, and who is one of yours.

Since the beginning of the world there were two energies. The first one was God, and after that came the negative energy of God. This negative energy was important because its purpose was to brighten God's power with its opposite power. God kept the negative energy away from His light so that His light could become brighter. When the light had been glorified, so was the darkness that was the opposite of the light. When God created a human being, He created the human being's spirit. He gave the spirit an opportunity to become glorified and placed the spirit near darkness. After God had created the spirit, the darkness wanted to create his own, and so it did. God created a home for the spirit, and that was the spirit body, also known as the astral body. The dark master also wanted to create a body, and so he did. His creation was evil and primitive, and his angels were demons. God created paradise, and He created a being like paradise man. They were our forefathers, not yours, Children of The Earth.

We were tall and beautiful, and we did not have a mind. We were very spiritual and intelligent, and we never did evil. When we were in Paradise, this evil energy came amongst us. He was as beautiful as we were, and he was one of us. He came amongst us like a serpent. We did not know that this evil had come into our midst, and we trusted him as we trusted our own. He created for us his brothers, the human being.

He created his own human that was short, rude, and not as intelligent as us. He did not appreciate God's creation but wanted to be equal with God in everything. God allowed it because it had to happen so that imperfection would perfect itself. God said, "Whoever believes in Satan and follows him will have to reincarnate, and he must suffer, and through pain to come back to God". Four of us left and followed Satan, and one of them was Lea.

Human beings were given a spirit from God, but this spirit was in trouble. The human being was not able to be in contact with the spirit as we were. What else could we have done but leave and go away? We left Earth to Satan and his angels. However, it was not the time yet where we would be completely gone.

Lea was given a second chance. She now lived in the pharaoh's court as the pharaoh's wife. The pharaoh was her soulmate, and he had never fallen into temptation. Once again Satan came and moved freely everywhere. The Sons of God were pharaohs, and they maintained spiritual power. They kept the secrets from the time when Satan himself created humans hidden in pyramids. They dominated energy and were in contact with God.

High priests guarded the tombs, and crazy was the one who wanted to seek the secrets of the tombs. One of the fallen angels was a high priest. He was one of Satan's helpers, and each of his students were working for Satan as we have explained. The Pharaoh could not do anything to prevent the evil that had entered his court. Satan's high priest started a new direction on how to keep the secrets of the tombs. He started to disturb spiritual development with his teachings and began to conjure demons.

The Pharaoh's wife was beautiful, intelligent, and she wanted to know what was going on in the tombs of this mummification master. The pharaoh cried, and tried desperately to prevent her, grinding his teeth he said, "Do not go to Satan, do not make a mistake again, you did it once and you were forgiven." Lea could not believe that the high priest was an assistant to Satan himself. She thought the man was different and had a curious charm of which her own kind did not possess. Lea left although the pharaoh was crying. He knew what would happen. Lea said, "I am only the wife of the pharaoh, I want to be a high priestess as well. I want to know what is going on, and I want to know what this new direction is." Lea wanted to know who this new mummification master was and this new direction. Lea left her beloved pharaoh and began her studies to become a high priestess. Soon she realized what was going on, cruel and mean was the high priest who was teaching her. His secret fire, water, and earth spells brought demons that wanted to conquer the temples and its disciples. Lea realized too late that she was being taught by the Devil. She wanted to end it and return to her beloved husband. However, nothing could undo what had already happened. She had to choose either to continue, or to be buried alive. She chose to be buried alive. The pharaoh's pain was greater than her pain, she would have to defeat Satan in her grave before her death.

There was nothing that could have saved her, yet she was given a third chance. Now she was in space, the commander of her own ship. She was beautiful and intelligent, everyone near her loved and respected her. Her beloved daughters were also on this ship and worshipped the commander of the ship. Life on earth was primitive and dangerous. All space humans knew that anyone who would come in contact with Earth humans could no longer live. All evil about human beings was known, and evil was at its peak on Earth. Sacrificial altars were being used to sacrifice and torture, and all of Satan's inventions had been discovered.

There was a war in space, Satan and his angels were at war with the Sons of God, but the war that was being fought then was the only one that ever took place on top of the sky. Lea's ship was hit, and she had to make a decision, either destroy the ship with its crew, or fall to Earth. She chose to preserve life and once more wanted to know what was going on Earth. This time she also sacrificed all those who loved her. What happened to her loved ones was worse than death. They were chewed to pieces by crocodiles and other Earthly predators. They could never again be as they should be. The evil had contaminated them with pain and negativity. They had to go with Lea and begin their reincarnations on Earth. (Privately written for Lea, "If you do not believe all of this you can be hypnotized, and you will find the same information from within you.")

All of those who loved Lea were less fallen, and their lives were often easier than hers. Lea was not allowed to meet with them very often, she was forced to live many lives like this one, completely alone and without love. In her current life, Lea met two fallen Sons of God who are Satan's own. One of them was her husband, whose life's work was to destroy her. The second was a practitioner of black magic who tried to seduce her with his spells. Lea never had anyone to help her, even her own daughters turned against her when it was time to take a stand.

In this life she had finally learned something. She no longer wanted to know Satan's secrets. She did not want to sacrifice those she loved, instead she sacrificed her own life for them. She had to choose a man who was her worst enemy. This was her sacrifice to make amends, and for this evil man, it was the last chance to make amends and change. After all, he was still one of us. Her atonement sacrifice was also to reveal Satan's secrets. She had to live cursed and live a life in such circumstances where she had no one to help, to understand or appreciate her. Although her life was difficult, as were all her previous ones, she returned to God, and soon she can live amongst her own.

Children of Earth, you cannot continue to do what you are doing to each other much longer. When the time is full, there will not be another chance. The grave is already open, and it is waiting. When the time is full, without any spiritual growth, you will be nothing but a corpse feeding the maggots. Many have found a religion. Who is their high priest? Is it Satan's accomplice from the tombs of the pharaohs? You cannot believe in a human being if you believe in God.

God is, in no circumstance, under the control of a human being. He is not as you want Him to be. He does not judge, He does not force, and He does not threaten. Jesus never said that it would be enough just to believe in His body. He said, "I am the way, the truth and the life, no one comes through the Father except through me." Nobody can be saved by repeating His name. He showed a path that will take you away from Satan. You must live on that that path. Crying and screaming will not save anyone, it will only scare away little children who will never again want to know about a man named Jesus. When your time is full, you will not have another chance. If there is no spiritual growth in you, you will just wither away, and nothing can help you anymore. You must be different when you die than what you were when you were born. Some will become evil from their life experiences, and some will become good.

Life is an opportunity,

to learn how to love,

learn how to know God,

learn from your mistakes,

learn to help others,

learn from Satan.

Satan himself created your body that is full of temptations, and in this body your spirit is in trouble. Your mind is from Satan, where he whispers evil things. We call this Satan's telepathy. We also produce telepathy. Our telepathy comes from the spirit. We do not cause harm, nor do we abduct people to our space craft. We do not conduct experiments, and we will not show ourselves to you. We have space crafts, and we could come and allow ourselves to be seen if that would be necessary. Our ships are large. Those that you love are not Men, (Sons of God) they are others, they conduct experiments, and they take people into their ships and do cross breeding. They are trying to refine the human race, as well as preserve human evolution. They live on their own planet, and they are not rulers of the spirit. They are not evil; they are just different, and they want to preserve human history. When the Earth falls, they will come and take human beings away, just like Noah did in his time. They want to understand what type of conditions humans can survive and how much psychological stress a human being can handle without going crazy.

A human being's consciousness is very low, close to an animal's consciousness. Only by spiritual development human beings are able to expand their consciousness. At the lowest level, a human's consciousness is slightly lower than that of an animal. At the highest level, a human's consciousness is slightly higher than that of an animal. A human's sexuality is dominant, during general anesthesia many have said that all they want is to enjoy sexual experiences, regardless of how they achieve them. No animal degrades to such behavior. Human beings must learn how to control their urges. Many people cannot even think about what is really going on in their lives. Some think that when they come to Heaven, all they have to do is say, "Jesus," and all will be well. No other being is able to lower itself, only the human beings that Satan created can do that.

However, we will not leave you. Although, you are not as we wished you would be. We will leave you a message and a lesson. We will explain that you should not wish in vain for the Sons of God to come and take you. You must be worth it for us to even want to meet you. We are not cruel when we explain to you who you are. We can never be as cruel as you are because when you love madly, your love becomes satanic. How can you think that someone who has been loved wants to die? How can you think that you are highly spiritual when everyone you know is in trouble and wants to die? How can you believe that you are intelligent when you cannot tell the difference between who is intelligent and who is not, and when you do not know if your priest is Satan? How can you believe that you are intelligent when all that you know about your bodies is that you have reproductive organs, and that you want to eat and complain?

We hear your prayers; we know who you are. We have all the information about you. When your body runs out of time, you will get what you deserve. Some of you will never return. Some of you are like dry wood that will be thrown in four different directions,

one part for Satan,

one part to the Earth,

one part to the state,

and one part to the ones who can never forget the evil you did to them.

A-A-A

Lea when you are asleep, we come to you and put this what we must. Lea only this is important, don't care what others say or do, if you don't mind, we will begin this work.

Only those who have abandoned God are truly evil. We don't want you to think that we are evil, we are not. If you want to come with Men, you could now, we begin.

Provided that you think we are others who you have met, we are not, provided that you want to come with us you can, if you want. Although here on Earth there are many good people, many are evil, and many have had mean thoughts about honest Lea. If you want to come to us you can but you don't have to. Lea, Men are tall, and we have a lot to say to people who want to know the truth. Lea, you want the truth, and you will be given the truth. There are many of us, not all are good, like the ones you saw on TV, they are not us. They are also tall, and they want that our own Lea would take them, if you would take them, they would only explain that Men are more evil than they are. Men have been a lot here with Lea and only want that you take those who have something important to say. Men are tall and we are fun, but not everything is quite what it seems.

We are Sons of God and we do not want to harm you. We are good and we have to come to people in secret because they are not the way they should be. They only know one way to live. They do not want any big changes in their lives. They think everything that is different is evil. They do not even understand that if evil comes, it is Satan, and when it does come, they will not even know what happened. If you do not understand what Satan is, you will not know how to live. You do not understand what is good and what is not, what you had, and what you have lost. You cannot comprehend changes, and you do not understand what is truly fun and what is not.

Although there is something here that we do not want to talk about. We do want to explain to you that your time has come to an end, it has come to an end. Taking many that were good away from here (Earth) destroyed many who had a lot to teach. Unfortunately, you did not want to have the opportunity to hear the truth. We do not know what to do with you human beings anymore.

We will begin this telepathy on behalf of The Great White Brotherhood *(* Not to be confused with White brotherhood. The Great White Brotherhood, in belief systems akin to theosophy and New Age, are said to be perfect beings of great power who spread spiritual teachings through selected humans. The members of the Brotherhood may be known as The Masters of The Ancient Wisdom, The Ascended Masters, The Church invisible or simply as the Hierarchy…etc. Wikipedia) for all of those who are in the light, and for all of those who will begin work on behalf of The Great White Brotherhood. There is something very dark here on Earth. Something that we do not want to touch. There is evil amongst you, and your thought processes are wrong. If you have never thought about what could happen to you when you chose not to think about things, we can only say that there is nothing more we can do.

Time has come to an end. If you want to be like one of Men, you have to learn one important thing. We are not saying that life is easy, but what is? The truth of living life is that it is a school. It is a school where you have a choice between good and evil. When you do not care about who and what you are, you are not part of this school. When you do not care about what kind of life you live, and that your only interest is to have fun, you cannot be a part of this school. Everyone who is here through difficulties are a part of this school. Honesty is one of the most important parts of this. If you cannot be honest, there cannot be much light in you. A dishonest person cannot be in the light. This also means that you are on the path of The Four Fires. If you have not burned in the fire, and do not know what that fire is, you cannot be in this school. This is a school for those who live in the light.

A funeral is already waiting for you. You want your funeral to be like your life. If you only want things that are not meant for you, you might lose the chance to be a part of this school, just because you wanted the things that you cannot take with you when you die; things that were not yours to have in the first place.

A-A-A

Lea, we can explain the truth. Lea, what is the truth? Explain the truth about Men. What is telepathy? This is telepathy. It means that you can be in this moment. We will come to you when you sleep, and you can begin the telepathy when you want. We can also be in direct contact. We are not evil. What is it you wanted to know?

Lea: "Who are the tall men in black hats?"

We will begin this by explaining that they are not who we are. They are others, whom you do not want to meet. They are not fun. They are not good. They are evil.

Lea: "Are they also tall like you are?"

If this is what you want to know, then we will explain what this is about. They are those Satan's sons who were once of us. They can come to Earth if they want. They are looking for their wives, wives who are still here on Earth. They are evil like the others, the ones you saw on TV. They wanted no one to talk about them. We have never said that to Lea, we have never said that you could not talk about us as much as you wanted and explain whatever you want, but we have never said that you cannot talk about us.

Lea: "Do you look like them?"

How can we explain, they are not quite like Men, would you like to see us? We can show ourselves to you.

Lea: "How?"

We will begin contact when you are ready to meet us. Maybe you should think about if you are in the light or not. What we are trying to explain is that there are many different vibrations that can also come through. If you were not different and pleasant, you might not understand how this world is. We are trying to say that you would not know who is who, had you not understood that there is an evil kind, as well as a good kind.

We talk about everything that is on Earth. Life on earth is a school. Life is your school, and although you do not want to think about it, one day we will not be here to help you. When the time comes when we are no longer here, you will be in big trouble. During that time, evil will be released, and you will have no one left here to help you. This means that we are still here, and we still want to help you, and we want to leave you a message.

Begin by repenting, because the time that is near means that time has come to an end, when nobody can have another chance. If you do not want to repent, and instead you continue to do evil, there is nothing we can do to help you. We will leave for now, but we will come back soon, like art we will leave. What is art? It is something that was created, and will remain, but the artist whom it came through is gone. We cannot be closer to you than we already are because you are not in the right frequency with us.

If you want telepathy like Lea, then be more like Lea. She only wanted to become one with what already is a part of her. She wanted what we wanted, for everything that happens only to happen so that we can learn from it, and that we are responsible for our actions by being willing to pay the consequences. We must think that the many things we cannot have is because we do not deserve them. Like every day we have a fish on the hook, if it falls when it should be lifted up, then it does not belong to us. That is why we cannot lift it up.

There are a lot of things about life we will not touch.

We cannot be anything other than who we are.

We are not claiming that the reason we began this work would be that if you do not learn through this, you will never survive from here and be free.

We are explaining this to you so that you can have peace when you want to be good and you cannot find Jesus.

Jesus was the way, the truth, and the life, but how many have misled people away from God in His name. Many were lost and then they found Jesus, and soon people came and said things to drive them away from Jesus. Not everyone wants to believe in another human being. Many are only searching for God.

We have a message for those who are still seeking telepathy. We do not want you to try this, and we do not want you to do anything that has already been done. After this, we will only continue with Lea. We will do this work with her and continue to be in contact with her until the end. She is one of us. She knows how to do this and to achieve this was not easy. For this to be able to work successfully, we had to work hard together. If you want to be the chosen one instead of her, we cannot help you. We come to her at night and speak to her. She does not remember this, but she is always willing to come to us.

She never said that we have fun here, she does not want to live here with us, but she comes with us because it is what we want. We never said that she is an angel or a prophet. She is simply who she is meant to be. All of her previous reincarnations were difficult, and she has a temper. In many ways she is like a human. When she was young, she had many problems. If you cannot reach her level of consciousness, you will never understand who she is. She will remain forever. Any similar messages that will come through after her will only be from the others. Lea has to be alone throughout this difficult time. Because she is strong, she has to survive all of this and be alone. Others have their own, but she is alone, and she is teaching you that, loneliness is better than to be with an evil person. Unless you say she is not who you want her to be, then she can teach you, unless you believe she will not come to you and explain, we don't explain everything at once, she knows how to think independently, provided that it comes through prayer, if not it is what it is. (Lea, although we say all this about you, you can continue to live your normal living life.

We do not want anyone to change anything that you do not want. We only want you to practice knowledge* and pray when you begin this telepathy. When you are ready, we can continue this work.)

    * Knowledge is a meditation technique, taught by Prem Rawat, that Lea practiced during her entire life.

A-A-A

Lea, the Men are here, and you can continue when you are ready.

Men start.

Jesus started here in heaven for the preparation of His teachings so that He could come down to Earth and teach you through His living life. He was one of the Men, He was just closer to God than any one of us. He gave His life for the most difficult mission on Earth. Had He not done that, nobody else would have. He had to put everything He had into the work that was hard and difficult. His life was so short, and He could not prevent the evil that did what it did to Him. He had to allow all of that evil to happen and He did not even have karma. Why can't you human beings be aware of what is happening on earth? Why is it that you do not want to know? Why do you continue to condemn those that are already in hell, to hell? Nobody can exist in a way that the way they were in the beginning is the way they will be in the end so do what you can, no one is able to prevent life and no one prevent how to live but what you can prevent then do that.

Hell does exist, and in due time, everyone will get their part of it accordingly. Why would you want to beat someone who has already been kicked and beaten?

We do not want you to talk about Jesus unless you understand what He wanted to teach people. He came to Earth and spoke about love and hope. He wanted to teach you a path away from Satan. After He had sacrificed His own body so that everyone who is searching could believe in what He said, He left. What do you want to tell Him? That He was not one of Men, and that He was not even a living human being? He was a man like Men are, but with His spirit, He overcame His desire for His own body. He overcame His desire to be one. He only wanted to give justice to everyone who had no justice. Like all the babies, and all the children, and all those living without any rights, in whose life other people can do whatever they want. He wanted for everyone who had been in contact with Him to continue to do the work that He did. He helped the blind, the crippled, the sick and the poor. He helped those who had no rights in their own lives. Whoever wants to follow Jesus has to do what He did. Just talking about Him does not help you go to Heaven. It is not enough to be serious and talk about Jesus. You need to live the example that He gave.

Many have said that they have found Jesus, that they have been reborn in spirit, and that they have received spiritual gifts and so on. There is no rebirth that will help you unless you live as He did. He was not one to come and explain that what is not from me is from telepathy. He said that what is from me is from God, and that what is from your body is from yourselves. He never said that you could come and say that He is gone. He continues to exist. He does not have to be born to exist. He is everywhere, all the time. He knows everything you do in His name, but those of you that sin with His name on your lips, and sin through His body, are Satan's own. Nobody here, or on Earth, would dare to do anything wrong through His body or name if they are a part of God. All Children of God know that He knows everything that is being done. A lot of evil has been done with His second coming. Only the ones near Satan would dare to play with such things, after that, there will not be much hope left for them.

What you are is what you receive. Nobody who lives without sin is without sin. The only ones being born on Earth are the ones with bad karma. After you read the book from Egypt that has been here on Earth, it is one of the texts from the "Book of Dead", called, "The Coffin Texts".

In its beginning stories, it explains that even though you have been here before, and even though you will come back, the body is not your temple unless you purify it, and the spirit is not clean unless you purify the spirit. You do not understand that everyone living on this Earth is contaminated. Why can't you understand that you are not pure, no matter how holy you try to be. If you still cannot understand, and you continue to condemn others to hell, then maybe one day you will sit face to face with Satan. He will come for his own, just like we will come for our own.

We also do not want to judge you, and we do not want you to drive Jesus away from those who really need Him. If you want to be one to assist Jesus, then go there, where there is not a moment when you can rest without pain or deep anguish. There are many of them, and their cries of sorrow fill the entirety of space. Why won't you help them? You just talk to each other about how you will come to the Kingdom, and how good you are. We do not care about that. We only want the ones who want to help, and who take away pain and sorrow in which the Children of the Earth are drowning in. What is wrong with you Children of the Earth? When you leave your children alone and go out to have fun without them, why are your children alone and why do they want to die? We do not want you to want us to come and send you telepathy. You have already been here long enough. You should know that this planet is not in the hands of God.

If you want to get away from here, then repent. You cannot leave from this Earth and think that it will be all over now. Nothing will be over unless you yourselves have done something to change that. What you think is the truth, is not the truth. Pray so that the truth will be revealed to you. Then perhaps one day it will be revealed, and after it has, you would wish it was not. Provided that you do not want to come and repent to change this living life, you might not get another opportunity. Maybe this living life will be your last and the time has come full.

For many their time has come full. That is the reason why there is so much evil on Earth. Many are here for their last time. There is nothing left of them after life and they know that. They want for many others to make the same choices they have and will do their last evil deeds. If they are one of our own, be careful. They are very dangerous. They are mean, rude, inconsiderate, and very intelligent. They know exactly what they have done, they do not care about anything anymore. The only thing they want is to get our own. They try to mislead all of those who have been reborn to change and change their way of life. If you have dealt with a person like that, be extremely careful. You cannot get rid of them, they know how to keep in contact with their victims, never letting them go.

We cannot prevent that; we can only warn you. There is a lot of evil here on Earth, and always has been. If you do not know who is evil, you will soon learn. Evil is evil, their thoughts, their actions and everything that they are is evil. If you do not know your brother, then maybe you do not know who he really is. Your brothers cannot be forced to reveal themselves, but when you keep God close to you, and you want to be near Him you will get closer to the truth. Nobody who is close to God can live in deceit.

Many are born to parents whose only mission is to destroy the child. It is the hardest karma that one can receive. After you have survived such karma, you have reconciled a lot, which means you have defeated Satan. If you do not want to believe that your own parents wanted to destroy you, you will never defeat the karma that you were given. You will have to be willing to let go of everything if you want to defeat Satan. Jesus did say to respect your mother and father. You can still respect them, although you abandon them. You can respect the fact that they fed you and took care of the needs of your body, but if they beat you, sexually abused you, broke your will, or if they did not love you, you will have to come to terms with that, and leave them. It is a serious crime if you are still trying to love someone who tried to destroy you. This means that you are trying to love Satan, and nobody who loves Satan is able to love God.

Jesus came on Earth long before all of Satan's works were known. Nothing was as open as what Satan did. So that he could be a good father, his children have been devils since the beginning of the world. They seemingly take good care of their children, and in secret do all of their evil. We were not always aware of everything that took place. Although we were given a lot of telepathy and were allowed be involved in many things as witnesses, not all things were clear for us either. All of the works of Satan are against the body and the spirit. We cannot take the evil away unless you fight against it. Do not keep Satan's secrets to yourselves. When you have been victimized, reveal those who did it to you, reveal all of those who are working for Satan and banish Satan away from everywhere it has come. If it is in your home, drive it away, if it is in you, cast it out, and if you do not know how, look for help until you find it.

Sometimes it is karma, bad karma. Maybe in some life you called for Satan, and Satan came. When he did, you no longer wanted anything to do with him. If you are not ready to start a spiritual life, you may never be ready. Start your spiritual life today. Maybe today is your last day. We also want to tell a story about an old man who had died, and who had never thought that spiritual life existed. He had worked and lived his life for ordinary material things. He was not a bad man, nor was he good. When the time came and he died, he did not die after all. With his astral body he attached himself to a nearby drunk.

He took over the drunk man's body and went to his own funeral. He kept avoiding the thought that he had died. He went inside his casket and tried to get back into his old body that was now rotting, and he started to live in there. The body was already in a casket and the casket was underground. He tried to get out and he was scratching and screaming. He ended up living inside his rotting body until the body deteriorated. After that, he began searching for the drunk man again. He found the drunk and went back into his body. Now he wanted to get back to his old home. The people at his house kicked the drunk out, but the dead old man did not leave the drunk alone. He kept on forcing the drunk to keep going back to the house again and again. Until one day, a man who had often beaten the drunk, shot him. Now there were two deceased in one body, back in the grave.

Together, they searched for another drunk. When they found one, they forced the new drunk to go back to the house. When another sick drunk showed up at the house, the people living in the house began to worry. They decided that the drunk was possessed and put a curse on him. Now, terrible things started to happen. Both deceased were in the hands of Satan. The one who was not good or bad, was now with Satan. Simply because he never had any spirituality. The man's soul was now in the hands of Satan and he had to go to Hell. The poor thing was very confused because he did not even realize that he had died. When Satan came to him, he asked, "How do you like your new fun home?" The old man placed his hands in prayer and said, "Now that I have cited my prayer and my body is burning, and I cannot find my way out of here. Can I please go back to my old grave site?" When Satan heard this he said, "Dear man, why would you want to return to your old grave site? There is no body, not even a casket left. What kind of wish is that?" The old man was in Hell and all he wanted was to return to his grave site. Satan said, "Why don't you want to go to Heaven if God hears your prayer?" The man looked at Satan with contempt and replied, "What kind of man do you think you are if you do not believe in how great God is? Better yet, if I cannot go where I want to go, at least I should be able to go to my grave."

Satan now tried to explain to him that he is dead and does not even own his own grave. The man said, "What is wrong with everyone? How stupid can you be to you think that you are Satan?" The man could not stay in Hell anymore because Satan thought that he was as stupid as the doors of Hell itself. The old man left Hell. He was now wandering around, not knowing where to go. Eventually, he ended up back in Hell and asked if he could come back because he did not know what else to do. Satan declined, saying, "No thank you, you are not worthy of hell."

Nobody has ever been saved from evil like this, by being worthless to Satan. Once again, the old man did not know what to do. He roamed aimlessly. As he kept wandering, he ended up shifting away from the lowest plane and began to search for others that were like him. When he did find others, they began to wander together. Finally ending up in a place called, "Help us, we don't know where we are!" There was an angel who was guiding the lost spirits. The old man wanted to talk to the angel. The angel was in the light. She was beautiful and only the man could see what was happening. The angel started to explain to the old man that he had died and should now come with her so that he could be lifted from the horrible dark fog in which he was in.

The old man did not want to believe the angel, saying, "I'm not dead, how could I be since I'm here?" He then said, "There was somebody else too and he claimed to be Satan. I could not even get into my coffin. I am not dead, and I don't believe in some Satan, and I don't believe in angels, nor do I believe in God."

"What do you believe in then?", the angel asked. He replied, "What I believe in, is that I can lay in my coffin. Nobody will allow me to do that." The angel now tried to explain that to be able to have a coffin, you would have to be dead, but the man would not have it. "Step down now and go wherever you wish to go then. Whatever it is that you want you can have.", the angel finally said. "To my coffin, that is where I want to go." After, he said that he was back in the coffin, and could be there until he was no more.

Perhaps this story will sound strange, but it is not that strange after all. It is a true story, but what truly is sad, is that he was not even a bad man, he was just stubborn. If you still want to be as stubborn, nothing will stop you. You are allowed to be free and choose your own destiny. We are not saying that if someone has once chosen Satan they could not repent. We have many who have gone to Hell and have eventually been able to come back up and continue the path to pay their karma. But any living life can be the last, where there are no more opportunities. Only those who are very materialistic and who only think about money and work are really in big trouble.

Lea, you are in cooperation with us, what is the Path of the Four Fires?

This means that you have been in each of the four fires, that in a sense, are like purgatory.

You have burned in four purgatory fires in this lower-level life.

You have burned in passion.

You have burned in love.

You have burned in hatred.

You have burned in pain.

The fact that you are alive means that you have survived it very well. This was not an easy living life as you know. Now that you have passed this, you have been purified from all of this. Without burning you cannot be purified. We do not want to talk any longer. Pray now, and we will begin again tomorrow, sleep well.

A-A-A

Lea, nothing is new in this world, all that was, still is. Old thoughts and old things are repeated, time does not change much. That is why it is important for people to change. Unless any change occurs, development cannot continue. It is development. As far as spiritual development is concerned, it is subject to the same laws. We all must change; we cannot stay at the same level. Unless change occurs, there is no growth. Although life is always very difficult, people never care that we have to change so that life will become easier. Why don't people want to change? Maybe it is just safer to remain the same as they always were.

We read an article about a man who decided to change his entire life. He had been a very successful man, but when everything in his life kept on repeating, he wanted a different kind of life. He left his wife and everything he owned. He left his job and left with a woman who owned nothing and had no children. Together, they started to travel around the country. One day, he wanted to see his wife and children, and he wanted to meet his old friends and co-workers. When he went back home, nobody was there. His wife and children had moved away. His old friends did not live where they used to anymore. Even his job had relocated. He no longer could find anyone he used to love. He was angry and disappointed. He started to travel around the country again. After a while, he got sick and tired of this lifestyle and the woman he was with. He left her and started to search for a new life again. He found a steady job and he wanted a wife and children again. He wanted a wife baking in the kitchen, and children waiting for him to come home from work. But what happened after he got tired of his family and left to change his life? He did not even know himself. He said that he was a nice man, but was he? Wasn't he inconsiderate and irresponsible in regards for other people's feelings? He was not an innocent man when did not care about what happened to his wife and his children.

When we say that you must change your way of life, we do not mean that you should do what that man did. What we are referring to is that you do not make the same mistakes over again but learn from your mistakes. When you make a mistake, learn from it. When you want to be loved, first think that you must be crazy if you do not know who loves you. If you want to know who loves you, get to know them first. After that you may think, is that the one you want to love? When you do not know what love is, think first, what do you want from love? Do you want the person who loves you to be reliable and serious? Or perhaps are they an old friend from a past life. If they do not respect you, then do not even consider them. That person is not for you. If they are just time that you cannot spend anywhere else, do not think of them. If they are not interested in anything that is important to you, do not think about that person. If they are pleasant and loving, but not trustworthy, do not think about them. And if you do not like that person, and just want to sleep with them, beware, it is karma that can have a high price in which you cannot afford.

If you still do not know what love is, then learn.

There are many who never learned, and they have left for good.

Love is. Provided it is love, it cannot be forced.

Love does not come and go when you want, instead, you just love when you have to, but if it wounds you, then you will have to end it. Provided that the love is not real, you must end it, and if you are not capable to love as you should, you must end it.

When we want to be happy, we will wait for helpers to bring him or her to us. We are not like you; we do not just take anyone because we are lonely. We wait until we find someone who is right for us. This is usually someone who is in the same frequency with us and their aura is in such a vibrational level that we do not cause harm to each other. When we begin our life together, we stay together until the end. After we have lived through that relationship, if we continue to have love for each other, we can meet again in our next life. Like we have explained, each has their own soulmate, just as we have. Often, however, we also are not allowed to meet them. We must wait as well, so that our aura can be together with our own pair. When the time has come, we will be able to meet, if we are ready.

When we are growing up, we do not even know who we are. First, we must learn to know ourselves. The best way in which we learn is through others. As we begin our relationship, we must be careful not to wound each other. When we grow apart, and we are not who we used to be in the beginning, the relationship will end. However, if the other one is still willing to continue, we need to take that into consideration. When the time comes to separate, we do not judge each other's feelings.

When a human being continues to develop, they keep on changing all the time. In a relationship, if the other one is not a part of this change, it might be so that the other person must continue alone. If the hunger for the other person is endless, or if that person is the only one that you can even consider, again the reason might be karma. External factors do not have an effect on true love. If one loves another, they no longer care how that person looks. It is replaced by a powerful feeling, where the only thing that matters is that you can be near this person so that you can feel their vibrations. Even long conversations are meaningless, the only thing that matters is that you can be near this person with whom you can be in a state of happiness and have a feeling in which you can rest. This happens because of the vibrations that occur when they are together, both of their auras are in such a vibrational level that in a sense they get intoxicated by each other. When they can be together, they will become very happy, but if they think that they cannot be together as lovers, then they cannot be together at all. This is why they cannot choose what to do, they have to be together as a couple or not together at all.

If love suddenly ends in a relationship like this, it is due to a re-birth, and when the living thoughts begin to create a disturbance in the peace of their auras. Re-birth indicates a body part that is located in the middle of the body, mind and the spirit. In this space a process can develop where spiritual development can suddenly grow so great that the vibrational level of the aura will change. This is a permanent change where its process cannot be stopped. If this happens, the other person is in a way, left alone in this sleeping process. They suddenly realize that they have fallen out of the harmony that existed since the beginning. This happens often and it will end many relationships quickly without any apparent reason. If the human being is spiritually developed enough, they will understand what has occurred. However, if you want, you can continue to live in the relationship, given that it provides enough friendship. It might be a very lasting relationship although you cannot find happiness as a man and a woman. If the relationship is only a friendship, it does not provide many sexual feelings, provided that they operate under the natural law. Long lasting relationships that are solely sexual are not love relationships either, and are often karma, provided that the two are very different and do not have much in common. Karma will be revealed when the relationship will develop a lot of problems that cannot be otherwise explained.

The relationships between a man and a woman are not always easy, even if they are, there are always risks involved. Very often they are not much fun although human beings are very enthusiastic about them. Regardless, it is important to remember that the parent's choices should never cause suffering to the children. It is essential for children to have both a mother and a father, that is why you should be very precautious when you want children so that your decisions do not cause them pain. Once you already have children, and the love is suddenly gone, then you must find the love. In other words, you must be like an open book that can be filled with new pages and maybe on the next page you can find love with this person. Humanoids are not like the Children of the Earth; we do not take and then leave the spouse whom we have chosen.

We will begin this story called, "Who Am I?" This is a story about a woman who wanted to find the man of her dreams. She did everything she could to be funny and beautiful enough. She knew how to be good and intelligent, and she knew how to dress in a way so that everyone admired her. Humanoids met this woman and we wanted to get to know her. We realized that this woman had never had even one person who loved her. She had all of those things that other people wished they had, and all of those things people wish the ones they could seriously love would have. Why didn't anyone love her? There was nothing she could do, she just waited for the right man to come into her life. When she was older, she gave up hope. Why didn't anyone fall in love with her? This was due to her karma; she had committed many crimes against love. In her aura there was such a factor that no one could love her, even those who would have been right for her. So not everything is what we want.

Whatever we explain, we can only explain partially. All things have as many different sides to them, as you have as human beings. We can only shine a little bit of light into the things that you do during your short life. You do not have enough time to learn. Our thoughts compared to your thoughts are too far from each other. The way we live is very different compared to the way you live. That is why, do not wish in vain that you were here with us. You do not show any level of development that could bring us together, but because of that you can begin a new world and maybe one day, you too may be closer to the paradise man who had all the elements needed for perfect happiness. We are not saying that you cannot be happy in your own way, but your happiness is not perfect. It is filled with revelations and white lies. The white lies are what you do not want to know.

We only want the truth. The truth will remain right regardless of what we want. When you learn to live on the Path of the Four Fires, and as you learn to become pure from the fire that has burned you, then you will come to a time where you can begin. This means that you have burned to become pure. Nothing leaves without being burned away, your sins must burn away.

About the law we were explaining, provided that you have not been purified, you will need to continue to burn, and after that when you have become pure, you are pure. Each one who has left from the Paradise are on the Path of the Four Fires. Each one who has fallen into sin is on the Path of the Four Fires. They will have to live their reincarnations, so that their original sins will be purified. The ones that have not started the purification are not on this path. They have chosen Satan, and they do not have to do anything but evil. As for the Children of the Earth, they are also subject to their own choices although they do not have to make as difficult choices as our own. Our own are subject to much harder choices because more is required of them. When you have reached a point where you know who you are, you will begin making new choices again. If you still fall in love with the wrong person, and if you still want to be like others, then you will return to the beginning and you will have to face a new tribulation.

The ones walking on the Path of the Four Fires have to learn how to love right. They must know what love is and what kind is true love. When they choose a partner, they must know if this someone is right for them or not. They cannot be tempted anymore into a relationship that will cause suffering and that could prevent their spiritual development. Their relationship must be the kind that will develop them spiritually and cultivate love in such levels that this love will remain in their aura body and will not fade. Lovers like this have often lived many lives together. The love stays in the aura body, and instead of fading it will only continue to grow. Couples like this can also be very different from each other, but they will always have this living love both in their spirit level as well as in their astral level.

Provided that you understand now, love is never simple. It requires you to be very spiritually developed so that you can experience love as you should. Human beings often fall for the physical expectations they have of each other. Relationships like that are not long lasting even for a human. Provided that you have been in telepathy with Satan, you will receive a lot of misleading information about the person who you think you love. Satan is seeking for suitable victims for his own. When couples that are united by Satan find each other, it will really become hell. Evil will provide many problems. One issue that will surface is that they can never have a satisfying sex life. One of them will always be looking for a new affair and when one wants to be intimate, the other one does not. They do not want to spend time alone with one another. They do not want to start anything new together and they do not want to talk to each other about anything.

You do not know what all that means? It means they cannot be together, yet they are not able to separate. If they do separate, they will end up back together though they cannot be happy. They live in a kind of hell. The couples that are united by God are always free together. They are like two birds that want to fly to the same branch. They do not care about each other's physical bodies. When they are together, they are always together in a way that does not cause them to separate. When God unites two, they do not want to live apart, which means that they can separate, but it is not what they want. Couples that have to separate and have to be together are united by Satan. Sometimes couples cannot continue to be together. They try and try but in the end they have no choice but to separate. That can be caused by Satan. They cannot control any element in them that in front of God is free.

We do not claim that everyone who is beautiful is evil, or everyone who is unattractive is good. We do not want to say that, but we want you to think, because you fall in love with beauty against your own will, that this type of love is falling in love with beauty. Sometimes, that is all that it is, after you get used to seeing this physically beautiful person, you will realize that you have never loved them. There are many men who have gone crazy and lost their minds when falling in love with a beautiful woman, and many women who have gone crazy over a good-looking man. This is only being infatuated with beauty that you have not seen before. After you get used to that beauty the feeling is gone. This is why you need to stay conscious of everything that happens to you, preventing you from making bad mistakes just because you do not know yourselves.

Routine is not love, many are just used to living together and they do not want anything to change. The only thing that they are being faithful to is their way of life, however, they might be completely different types of people and one can be very unfamiliar to the other. Together they are like two strangers that no one else can know how to find. Couples like that are often very cold to each other. The only time that they will spend together is when they are with their children or when they have nothing else to do. Is it not better then to be alone? We will not give you an answer to that.

When you do not know what to choose, then do not choose anything. Allow the answers to come to you. When you do not want to be alone, it is better to learn how to be alone so that you will not end up making bad mistakes just because you are afraid of loneliness. When you want to have children then be in harmony and have patience. When you want to have children, they need both a mother and a father. Children will also need to be in harmony so that they do not get damaged. When you are not sure of what to do, then wait patiently until you do. Sometimes it is better to stop the pregnancy than to have a child in life conditions where they cannot be in harmony and they will have to suffer. Sometimes you do all that you can, but the karma can be so severe that it cannot be prevented.

Karma is karma, you do everything that you can, but things cannot be changed. Lea's life is a good example of bad karma. If she had made a different choice and not married the kind of man that she did, she would have had to love someone else that would have been like her husband was. She could not have prevented the karma that she had to pay. Provided that someone would have helped her, they would have been a part of her life from the beginning of her reincarnation, but she could never meet anyone like that. As we have explained, everyone's life is different, and you alone will have to find your truth. The truth cannot be explained to you by anyone else. Only things that have already happened can be explained to you. So, when meeting with someone who predicts life and the future they should only help you to better understand who you are, so that through yourself you will know what is best for you.

When you choose, you can choose wrong and consequently inflict pain on others. You are not the only one paying the price for your wrong choice. When choosing a spouse, if you choose one that was not meant for you, your choice took them away from someone else. When you have chosen the one that is meant for you, you have done what you needed to do.

If the relationship is unhappy and you are unable to end it,

it might be karma,

It might be satanic,

It might be anything else, but it is not what you are looking for.

In a successful relationship, the relationship can end and start again if something goes wrong. If you are still searching but cannot find what you are looking for, stay patient, what is meant for you will come to you. Nobody can take what is not theirs to take. Whatever you are searching for you will find, and whatever you do not want but will have, will be the one who is your own.

A-A-A

Men will begin this.

As we have explained, we do not think like you humans do. We have had a lot of telepathy from humans and we know how their thoughts are. We think about things. Angels do not have to think about things, they simply exist. They are spiritual beings, they love, and they help. They are Men's helpers. They help us so that we can do the work that we do. Angels are always near us and as needed we send them to you humans as well. They help so that you can feel better, and they help you to start your prayers, and they help you to get closer to Jesus, who came here on Earth only so that He could create a bond between humans and God.

Before He came to Earth there was no bond. Satan kept this planet as his own and everyone living here was in complete darkness. There was no way out. There was only suffering after suffering. That is why Jesus came. He wanted everyone who wanted at least one spiritual teaching to have one, so that everyone who wanted to receive at least one thought that God exists could have one. He wanted for anyone who wanted to change their way of life to be able to do that. He wanted for anyone who desired love to feel it. He gave his only life on behalf of loving everyone who wanted to love God. His mission was hard. He was a man like other men, and also wanted to live a regular living life. We still have all of His telepathy saved. We kept His each and every thought and saved them so that everyone who still wants to go down to Earth to help can know that life is not easy. Not even for the one who is as pure as God.

If you still doubt that we do not know what you or others think, then you do not know what telepathy is. Read the following. Unfortunately, we cannot explain what the future holds because it is against God's Law. Nobody is allowed to explain the future, not even us. We can explain to you who you are and why, and we can explain to you who you were, but we cannot tell you the future. The future you hold in your hands. If you want to become one with us, we have to be sure that you are the kind of spirit you need to be. We cannot take just anyone. When we cannot be sure we will send you a test that can be rather demanding, but it will tell us how you have developed spiritually. There is no other path. There is only path and only one truth, there are no two paths or two truths.

Although you love, you do not know how to love right. When you go to your loved one or when we come to you, how will you know who we are if you do not know how to love right. This is important. There is not just one, but there are a thousand ways of how to love, but only one way is right.

Many have drowned because of the spells of the water and fire. Many have been tempted to cast spells that they should not cast. In a sense, Jesus did spells, but these were from God that were not made in the darkness or anywhere unseen. Our flying crafts are not magic. We use electrical energy that originates from the sun and from space. This electrical energy gives us the ability to fly where we want to. This means that, provided one has the ability to control certain laws of space, they are able to use these energies. These different energies can only be used by us who are from God.

Satan introduced different types of satanic energies because he wanted to be like God in everything. He also sent his son to Earth who called his troops from space to come with him. They do not have any light or possess any light field like humans do. They live only on temporary terms. Provided that you meet them, you will immediately think that they are evil. If you are not careful, they can become very troublesome when trying to get rid of them. After an encounter like that has been established, you will be in trouble. Hawks and small predators are their symbols. Provided that you think that the hawk was a symbol in Egypt, it became the symbol in contemporary Egypt, where evil was already in control. Our symbol is the number eight, which means eternal. That is the symbol we send to our own. Our space craft is our symbol in today's world, but before that we used some animals that Native Americans used to explain certain things. A Stork has been one. A Stork symbolizes the new coming. Storks are the kind of birds that come when the time is full. Under that symbol, our own are born.

Our way of thinking is different from a human in many ways. We never want to cause pain to another being because we want something for ourselves, regardless of what that something would be. You humans do not care what another one feels. Whatever you want, that is what you will take regardless of how it will make others feel. We will never say that when we are in a relationship, and after our loved one has been away that we will soon begin the relationship again. We are in a relationship from the moment we are in contact with one another. We never leave our loved ones here if they have problems. Like you do, we have our problems as well. We will never have intercourse for the sake of an orgasm. We make love only because we want to be as one with this spiritual being in the same body. If we do not want to make love with each other, then we will not become a couple. We will not make mistakes like that. If we cannot find the one who would be right for us, then we would rather be alone. We do not want to cause harm to one another by having relationships that are not right for us. We want for everyone we are in touch with to be happy and independent. We do not want to make anyone dependent on us. Everyone is meant to be free. Under the Laws of God even the lower beings must be free.

We begin, what we begin.

Always be close to God. He is the only one who can help you. It is very important that you never cast any spells. In each spell there is magic that can prevent you from coming to God. This is one of Satan's methods to keep those who have fallen as his own. Even if you have cast spells and are now in a bad place, provided that you want to become free, you must begin by searching for someone who can help you. Some people say that they can help. In reality they are unable to do what they should. You must remain open minded and search. If God wants for you to be saved, then maybe in the end you will find help. All of you who have given up hope, why are you even reading this? If you have given up hope, then you no longer care enough to look for salvation. Provided that you still doubt, you can go to a church and listen to the priest's sermon. Maybe God wants to speak only to you. Maybe you do not want to believe this, but God is everywhere. He knows all the things that you do not know. He knows everything that was done to you, when you were little, and when you were a baby, or when you were eight months old and in your mother's womb.

Eight is our number, the symbol of infinity. Now is the time to explain what you have been waiting for. When time has come to an end, and the Earth can no longer go on as it does, we will come, and we will get all of our own. Those who were under the power of evil and those under the power of good. We will not leave those who are evil behind. When they are here, they will know all of their choices and each of their incarnations on the Path of the Four Fires. We cannot help those that believe in Satan to the end. We cannot, even though we would be willing to do that, but only so that we could prevent it from happening. When judgment comes, it will be the last one. Nothing will help them. When they realize everything at the last minute, it will be too late then, and everyone in that moment will know. When the time is full, those that are our own will come back to us, and those who are not ours anymore will go to the one that they have served. They will have to go and burn in such fire, that in the Bible is called hell's fire. They will live in an eternal fire that is Satan's own flame and it will burn into a grave until Satan's fire has diminished. Their telepathy will be like it is with Satan's own. They will curse and yell and scream horrible things. Their consciousness will be just a slight idea of themselves, but they are burning in a great fire that Satan has created for himself and his own. This fire is fire, but it is not like Earth's fire. It is an energy spirit whose mind is dark, black energy, and it comes from a fire whose only father is Satan.

Provided there was a time where nobody knew anything about the times of spiritual life, they will not be judged according to what they did not know, but everyone who does know, will also be responsible for this information. That is why if you still want to know more, change yourselves so that you are able to receive this information, and so that you can still continue to live your life as you are.

About a person whose thoughts are negative and judgmental, beware of those that want bad things, they are not in control of themselves. When someone wants horrible things, it is best for them to seek help from somewhere. If they cannot find help, they should go to a church or to someone who is spiritual. As soon as bad things take control of you, start thinking about what is wrong, something is wrong when that happens. When you act on your thoughts that are evil, then you are receiving telepathy that comes from Satan. Look for someone who is capable of helping you. Pray and search for help. When you start having outbursts of rage and severe eternal delusions, get in contact with a priest or a nearby spiritually developed person. It is an eternal delusion because you will think that you can comprehend the Storks and everything else at the same time.

Nothing that comes from us is like that. Men teach everything in small portions, the information cannot be received all at once. If it would, it would disappear immediately. Your brain is not capable of receiving everything at once, it is not possible even for our own. If you do not have anybody who can help you, as you know you have been given this telepathy. Through this telepathy your consciousness will expand, and you may momentarily experience something eternal. Take all the hawks and other small evil predators off your mind and come to Men. Send love to us, thoughts of love, like God's love. Open your mind, be in silence and allow yourselves to become empty and wait and see what you will receive. Maybe you will receive a message from Men that will help you. If you feel like you did not receive anything, or if you made it up, take it or leave it, but if you do receive a message from us, you will be very happy for a long time. That is what we can give. We can give you a good feeling. We are the senders of that feeling of happiness. However, if you are not able to receive happiness, then there something is wrong, and you will need to take a closer look at your life. Maybe what you need is psychological help instead of spiritual. You must learn how to separate these two. Not everything is psychological, and not everything is spiritual.

When you pray, pray in spirit, do not pray only with your words but instead, you need to seek your spirit, and with your spirit, you can send prayers to God. Provided you cannot find your spirit, try to find it from outside of your brain and mind. You will know that you have found your spirit when you have found it. When you do not have the strength to go on in life, then start everything from the beginning. All the things you have done have been wrong. You will have to find a new path so that you will be able to live better. When you are alone and you do not have anyone who loves you, then think of all of those bodies who will never have any hope to love, those whose bodies are not developed like yours is. The ones whose brain does not function properly, or those who are not even able to move their bodies. Their karma is horrible, you can go and visit them. They can still feel, and they can want things that they can never have.

Provided that you do not want to learn through prayer and through everything that you have been given, then you are not one of our own. Nobody can force you to continue, but you can choose to learn. When your living life is over, an angel of peace will come and say, "I am the one whom you have not met, would you like to come with me?" The spirit is alone and crying, "Everything is over, and I no longer have a body." If you are too attached to your body, then you will be in trouble. You will not be able leave your body that is still yours. This is a terrible moment for many who had worshipped their body, or the bodies of others. They are in big trouble with themselves, with their body, and the spirit world. The spirits want their aura body while they want their own physical body back, this can be a difficult time for many. The spirits do not realize that they are dead, and they will try to take over another aura body which would make them feel more alive.

When the angel of peace comes, they want to help, they will explain, "You have died and now is the time to leave your body that is no longer alive." If you have never been aware of anything, or never thought about these things, you will not be able to adopt the idea of how things are, and you will be in trouble. You will be in a grave waiting for relief. That is why it is important to became aware of these things before death. The angel of peace is a good spirit that wants to help. They are not real angels, but humans that have spiritually awakened, sometimes they can even be living.

Lea had done this work, and in a different way she met many who had passed away. She was there to escort some, and some she welcomed. They were all happy to go with her. She has done a lot of spiritual work. When the spirit moves on, it will arrive in a small space where it will meet with family members who have been waiting for this newcomer. Provided there is no one there to welcome you, crazy is the one who does not move on, because after this, an evil spirit will come. This is the kind of a gate where you will move either forwards or backwards.

On one side, there will be family, old spirit friends, or soul mates and so on, and on the other side, there is Hell where all the evil thoughts and works are burning. From this Hell, as we have previously explained, you are still able to get out and when the spirit does, it will be able to go back to the gate and back to his or her own. Satan does not care who leaves, as he usually gets his own back. There will come a time when you cannot go back and try again, if you are like the old man was in the story that we have previously told, then nothing can be done.

The old man did not want to go through the gate. Although he was in the light, he did not want to leave. Eventually he left the grave and found the light so he did not suffer all of that for nothing, but he could have remained on that path. There are many different opportunities, nothing is as hopeless as it seems if this is beginning to make you uncomfortable. So, when you leave here and you die, nothing is over. Provided that you can think the right way and are spiritually developed, then you can come back (reborn) much sooner. You might even meet those people who you want to meet instead of those who have very little importance in your life. Many things are connected to spiritual development, which is that you learn to live in contact with the teachings of Jesus, the Sons of God, and God.

A-A-A

(Lea we are here, and we can begin, Men are here, and we would like you to continue, we begin.

We will begin this work, choose only what you must. Lea although you were born under such laws, that you could be in a better position, you are still free so that you could find your identity.

We begin this work that must be done. The devil tempted you, because you have not been able to find a suitable companion, or any companion, it is not because you couldn't find company, but the truth is that you wanted to be free and alone that you could finish what you had to do. You thought that there was something in you that prevented you to find anyone, this something was you, you just didn't remember this.

Your aunt Elli had told you, she knew you were not any ordinary girl and she wanted to help you to understand, she gave you two books so that you could understand that your family had a bad curse, but everything that had happened, happened only because of what happened in Egypt, that was the reason why certain things happened, behind what happened was Satan himself whose helper was the black magician.)

A-A-A-A

Lea, today we will continue with this other subject. When we say that we are different from you, we mean that we are different in many ways. The lower self has been removed from us. We do not have different kinds of body parts like other humanoids, physically we are very similar to humans. With the exception that we do not have a lower self at all. When we say that it has been removed, we mean that it was removed from us since the beginning. It is a quality possessed only by the ones created by Satan. In a sense, it is a spiritual quality and not physical, and neither is the body that Satan created. We are speaking about the astral body. Men specify that from the beginning, ours, the space human's astral body, was different than the astral body of a human being with the absence of the lower astral body. When Satan created humans, he created the lower astral body, and this was the lower self-body, that is not like ours.

A human's physical body began its evolution being conscious. Satan started in his telepathy to create a physical body that was like ours. It just became much smaller, and unfortunately much worse. It continued to evolve until it finally reached the form that today's human has. God created us much like it is has been explained in the Bible. He made us from dust and from the beginning element. One of God's miracles is that He gave light to all the animals as well, and the best of all, He gave them an opportunity to continue to develop.

Animals have their own evolution, but contrary to what you have always thought, they will not evolve into a human. They will evolve into the Others. These beings who are the result of the animal's evolution, those you have met. They are not humans as you have thought, they are short with large eyes. They have realized that humans are destroying the evolution from which they have come from. They do not like the air traffic that humans have created because it disrupts the living life of all the birds and other creatures living in the air.

They want to protect all animals, and as needed they take humans with them to create cross breeding to refine their evolution. They want to make their own evolution such that they can live amongst humans and be closer to the animals that they want to protect. They also try to refine the human because humans are evil and unintelligent. We do not want to mix our genes with humans anymore because everyone who had our genes became worse. This was due to the lower self. This happened because the human that Satan created could not be like us because of the lower self, and as we refined the human genes, the lower self became even stronger and the human beings who had our genes became more evil. Unfortunately, by doing so we did a favor for Satan. Now we want to fix these terrible mistakes. We also want to help those that are our own and had fallen.

Satan's men are the kind that once they take someone as their victim, this person will be in big trouble. Lea was also one of their victims. They came to her every night, they looked like dark figures and they created paralysis like conditions, horrible fear, and they conducted all types of tests and wanted sexual things. They kept her in a bad state of mind. Usually, their objective is to put devices in humans and follow them. They search for the kinds of people they can use as needed, of course, they also want to find our own. After they left, they kept in contact with Lea. They wanted to keep her under their control, and they wanted her to go crazy. Once they left her, they left her alone for good. They are very evil, and their telepathy creates a dreadful feeling. They are not cat men although cat men are in the same wavelength, they are subject to different laws. Their qualities are that they influence low telepathy. They can come when someone has been inflicted with serious damage with low telepathy. The low telepathy comes into the low self, that everyone born a human has, each human has a low self, like everyone has a higher self that God created.

The human body has a physical part of the brain that we do not have. This part of the brain is called cerebellum, the sub-consciousness and the lower self is in this part of the brain. This part of the brain was created by Satan. The subconscious is not necessary if the human is sufficiently spiritually developed. We do not keep anything hidden in our brain. The purpose of the lower self is to keep all hidden information that the higher self cannot access and control. When this lower self develops, rage and other morbid conditions come from there and they will begin to live independently. This is how the satanic part of a human begins to live. Provided that the human being would learn how to take care of their own psychology and would not fail to treat psychological disorders, the subconscious could not develop to become independent. Many people suffer from obsessive behaviors that are created by the subconscious. Many rapists rape from a subconscious compulsion. Stealing and other evil deeds come from the subconscious as well. After the subconscious mind begins to store events, compulsive behaviors are born, it is crucial not to leave psychological issues unsolved.

This why you are so evil, you do not know how to control your bodies. Do not play with fire. Humanoids do not play games with their sexuality or participate in horrible orgies. These are all produced by the subconscious and the lower self.

Provided you want your wife to be happy, you can start this on a level where you truly love her. When you love her, she will want you to be as happy as she is. If you want to give the spirits what they want, then you want for them to remain in a lower level. The spirits want to be kept at a lower level because they still want to be alive, they want to be able to do all the same things they used to when they were alive. They approach people with different sexual needs. Many spirits still want to experience orgasms so they will go into a body that likes to have orgasms. When such a spirit has taken power, the human can no longer control their sex life. They are forced to continue to have orgasms, and if they do not want to, their subconscious will to force them to masturbate. Also, many evil spirits will come into a body that has strong sexual needs. Sexuality is a dangerous game; it is playing with fire.

We do not want you to take things lightly. You will have to pray in the mornings when you wake up and at night before you go to sleep. When you wake up and you have been out of your body, there can be a spirit in your body. That is why it is important to pray before you fall asleep. It is important to remember that unless you want your prayers to go to Satan, you must be in the light. As we have previously explained, you must find your spirit, and through your spirit your prayers can go to God. The prayer can begin very typically then suddenly become evil; this happens because of the filthy lower self's spirit that will surface when you try to pray. The lower self can be very dominant, it can also provide you with explanations that you do not want. It can explain that the people who you love are evil and so on. The small evil spirits that are everywhere are bodiless demons. They can create a lot of harm. They are small little creatures that do not have much intelligence. They would always go to Lea and torment her, hiding her personal items and so on. We had to drive them away, prayer will also help in banishing them.

When you do not want to be in Satan's telepathy and to be controlled by your lower self, first you have to became pure. This will not always be easy, if you have long dispersed your own idea of yourselves. There are angels in Heaven that you can call for help when you want to be purified. Angels can help with that. They come and contact the higher self and help it to get stronger in this battle that will take place in the human's own body. When you start this battle, Satan's demons will come, and this is how the spirit world is in war with one another. During this type of battle, one can experience difficult mental states as well as a feeling of a powerful love energy and have outbursts of rage. Love energy can have an effect in a way that the person will suddenly begin some type of charity work, despite the bad fire that the person is in, they will want to help others.

They cannot stop these outbursts, they are compulsive, but the person may also feel that they want to be enlightened. Some will feel an urge to hurt themselves and they want to harm their own body when they are in telepathy with Satan and the lower self. Self-destructive behavior is the result of the spirit only being aware of what was happening to them but was not being able to understand what is happening on a physical level. When the battle begins, it would be better if someone who has spiritual powers helps. The spirit who is fighting for its power is part of this battle. The spirit is not able to do more, and all other things will have to be set aside. This will become a very difficult situation for those without any help. This battle takes place in such a level that the human being is not aware of what is taking place. They might feel that they are controlled by different types of powers. When someone else witnesses this, they can feel a shift in vibrations from these energies. When you realize what is happening to you, do the following and stay away from other people so that the spirit who is struggling does not get too weak. When you are around other people it disturbs the battle. You can start a prayer for the sake of your spirit and ask God to send you more help.

Humanoids were in telepathy with a person who was in this fire. We helped this person and as a result he stopped using all the drugs he was using, and he no longer wanted to have sex without love. We connected with him because he was always talking bad about us, he would say that all humanoids and UFOs are nothing but bad imaginations. This was very peculiar because he was very irresponsible, however, his spirit was very strong and when he finally established connection with us, he asked us to help him. First, he did not believe that we were sending him telepathy. When he did understand, he was able to receive a message from the brothers that we were here to help and if he really wanted, we could help him. This does not usually happen, and we told this story about him because oddly enough we helped him, instead of one of our own.

Now that you know you have the opportunity to receive help from both the spirit world as well as us, you can begin to repent. We will help you if we are able establish contact. This would require that you be able reach the correct vibrational level. This is not always easy, although we know your thoughts, you must find your way to us. Without spiritual development, this usually does not happen. The lower self is frail, and it is not evil unless you speak to it and allow it to grow.

Humanoids have come to Lea every night and we have explained all this, she is just not able to remember it. We want you to trust us when we have chosen someone to do work with. She has been with us since childhood. We will not begin another mission after this work with her has been accomplished. After this, we will only send energy and messages directly at that level to whom is ready to receive it.

A-A-A

We are humanoids, we are the Sons of Heaven.

People are strange because they do not even know that they are evil. They think that if you do not do evil things then you are not evil, but not doing evil is not enough. Many that do not do evil things are evil because their aura is at a much lower vibrational level than others. They can live like any other regular person; they go to work, and they are ordinary, but they are evil. They are not spiritually developed and there is not a lot of light in them. After they die, they go to Satan because they are evil although they have lived a productive life. This type of evil is all Satan's own, and they will return to that energy when their time has come to an end. Their qualities are that they are insensitive and callous, and they do not possess any warmth, love or compassion, they can even pretend to have these feelings, but anyone who comes across them will know that they are completely cold. When they look for a spouse, they normally take one that they can benefit from. They just want to use people, unfortunately they have never loved anyone. They live their lives cold heartedly and they are evil spirits even if they did not do anything bad. They can even attend spiritual events and can even do charity so that they can better hide who they really are. They cannot be anything other than what they are. Provided that they want to heal and repent, they will have to find God quickly. Most likely if they pray, they pray to Satan and when they search for God, they cannot find him because they have lived too many lives as Satan's own. If they want to change, they will have to begin a spiritual cleansing that can take dozens of years. They cannot become clean from Satan just like that, they have to work hard to banish Satan.

We have worked with a man like that for twenty years and when he finally became pure, he was not who he was before. All his thoughts had been dominated by Satan. All he had wanted was money, sex, recognition, and power, all the other things Satan's own want. We will come to you when you call us to help you and when you do not want to be Satan's own anymore and when you realize that your life is completely wrong and that because of the lack of your own feelings you are unable to love anyone else. When the cleansing begins, you will have to renounce Satan. This will be a difficult battle and once it begins you must be careful not to hurt yourself or the ones living near you. When you realize what is happening in your life, start the spiritual cleansing. Your children do not love you anymore because you never gave them any love and therefore, they are not able to love you. They just want to use you like you had used them. When it is all over and you realize that you are evil and you want to change, you will begin by finding a highly spiritual person who can help you. They will need to pray in the mornings and at nighttime, they will also need to find a place where they can perform an exorcism, even if once a week. They will also need to start opening your thoughts. They must open your thoughts so that you will know what and who you are. You can even get psychiatric help in search of your true self.

If you are not open minded and honest then nobody can help you. You will remain evil. The only one who can help you is you. If you are not sure whether you are good or bad, you must study yourselves. Maybe you are not evil. Maybe you are just lonely, or maybe you do not have anyone close to you because you are too different. This often happens to our own. They are too different for anyone to be able to understand them. Evil people are different. They are not intelligent and different, they are cold, without emotions and they lack empathy. If you have met one like this, then you know what it is about. In their presence everyone will feel a deep cold in a way that cannot be described. They are spiritually undeveloped, and they seem level-headed. On a physical sense they can be very developed. Usually on a material level their affairs are in order and they may be very attractive. This happens because they are developed in their own way, and therefore, can choose which ever quality they can experience. Normally, the only quality that they wish to experience is automatically appearance.

Everyone who comes to life can choose certain qualities that they find important. Some think that intelligence is important, some want to be independent, and others want to be funny and so on. You are able to choose some of these qualities. Although you might think otherwise, not everything is karma. Appearance is very often karma, but once again some can choose to be physically attractive or to possess some other physical quality. These evil ones usually want to have a strong physique because they are otherwise undeveloped. When they can be attractive, they can try to find a proper victim that they can take advantage of. In a sense, they have a mission from Satan, they can seduce people who have other qualities. That is the reason why they are allowed to be who they are, so that God's Law can be fulfilled, so that there will also be temptations that we will have to learn how to overcome.

When a human must choose between two different people, and one is beautiful, and the other is a better choice, he or she will just have to know how to choose. When making a choice like that and you choose wrong, the consequence is usually rather bad karma, especially those who have prayed and then chosen wrong. It will be rather bad when you have prayed for a spouse and when you have to choose from two, and choose the wrong one, the relationship can become very unhappy.

After the old man has been burning in Hell, he returns to the angel and asks, "Where is that Heaven after all?" As the angel begins to explain what Heaven is, the old man says, "Whatever it is, it will be better than the place I was before." This is the way that a human being slowly begins to learn what they must.

Choices made against love are far-reaching. They can last from one living life to another, that is why you should think carefully about which choice is the right one.

Humanoids do not have this problem; we know who the person is that will make us happy. We live on a high spiritual level. We do not look at appearance or physical characteristics. Humanoids choose the one who is meant for us and we do not hesitate when we know the time is right and we have met them. Sometimes the couples can be very different. Sometimes one can be very beautiful, and the other very different. Things like that have nothing to do with our choices. After we have lived the life that we have and die, we will wait until we can come back. Now that we are here, we can start everything from the beginning. We know who we were in our past life, who we lived with, and everyone we used to know. When we meet again, we will continue from where we left off. Our level of consciousness is much higher than a human.

Sometimes our brothers have difficulties adjusting to our way of life. We then can place them on Earth. Like we have previously explained, that usually does not happen, but it has happened throughout history. Sometimes it just so happens that someone will spend a lot of time traveling in time, and they want to be able to live as a human. Some just want to live a life as a human because in their own way, humans are important. After they have defeated Satan, they can have a much higher position here among us. With us, they are in a much higher position. Together with those who have lived in biblical times, lived as women, lived as humans. They can spend an entire era away from life to be able to go and teach and guide others about the most important karmas known on Earth. Those were serious men that remained unmarried and knew when to remain silent when the time came. They were people who never stopped loving Jesus. After they had been sacrificed, tortured, and their mission was that they started, the Path of the Four Fires made them out to be stronger than Satan. Humanoids have not lived through that in life, we have not been near Satan and we never had to battle Satan like the ones living as human have. So, all our own, and those who were human and had defeated Satan, are in much higher position among us, however we are not angels.

Angels do not pray, and they are never born into skin and bone. As we have previously explained, they are spiritual beings that are as pure as God in Heaven. Their activities are such that they begin to create thought patterns where there is always only thoughts of God and Jesus. They create all the spirits of creation and they create all the spirits that are born to Earth in a human body. These spirits are not angels although they are produced by angels. These are the spirits whose purpose is to begin incarnations and then return to God. This is the spirit that the human being has, and over this spirit God and Satan battle over. All the beings existing on our lower levels are the animal spirits and then the nature spirits. They are spiritually conscious as well. Nothing that is alive is without a spirit.

Satan's spirit world turned into a low spirit, he became the low spirit, and all his demons are low spirits. The only purpose of the low spirit is to maintain the balance that God has created to be perfect. After that work is finished, embodied Satan will get a new task. In that sense he also is eternal, but the low spirits in which he controlled will disintegrate into him. Then again, beings of God will keep their independent existence and they can continue to develop to become even more perfect.

When you do not know Satan, then you do not know what evil is, and what is not. That is why you need to learn to know him. When you know what you do, and still continue to do it, you will be responsible. You will burn in fire when you choose evil after you know what it is. For this reason, you do not have to take the information and knowledge we offer. Once you receive this knowledge, you can no longer turn back and say, "I didn't know that was an evil thing."

Who is the one who wants to be a woman that will be taken seriously? This was Lea. She wanted to come here as a woman, only so that whatever she would say or do would for that reason be important. When she understood what it is to be a woman, she realized that the task she was facing was not an easy one. When she wanted to be heard, everyone said to her that she was funny, different, weird, and so on. She had to learn how difficult a woman's life is. She had to realize that a woman's life is much harder than a man's life, and that you still had to be a mother even after your children were adults. She wants for all the current concepts of women to be revoked and that women will receive respect as equal beings, just as all the men who have ruled this planet Earth.

Women's attitude is wrong. The love that women waste for a man is as useless as the sweet talk that men offer to a woman instead of love. There is no one who has been as patient as women, no man would ever be able to bear the burden of a woman. After all the pain and suffering women go through while taking care of their children, they also have the strength to pamper their men. Men do not even bother to spend time with their women but leave with the first temptation to seek a cheap thrill. Men must change as well as women.

You cannot continue with this attitude. Women should not love men who are not worthy of anyone's love, and men should not be looking for only casual affairs. When you do not want physical pleasures, you are searching for friends. Then you will find spiritual and intelligent people.

How can you say that you know how to love if you cannot love someone who is like how you think they are? Provided that you want to learn to love, first learn to know yourselves, and when you know who you are, then look for people that are like you. No woman can love a man who does not care about her. A spirit that does not care about another spirit is not the kind that you should be in contact with.

When you go back to the time when you were little and you were told that you were stupid because you were interested in sex, you started to feel guilt. This guilt will drive many into a state in which they cannot combine love and sex. Guilt drives people searching for one-night stands and sex without love. It is important to learn to unite love and sex. When you have learned that you will realize that you are much happier when you are able to have sex with someone you love.

Not everything is karma, karma is only the things that you cannot change no matter how hard you try. When you want to be happy and have done everything that you can, but you still cannot be happy, maybe it is your karma from a wrong choice you made somewhere. If you are still searching for happiness, you will finally realize that happiness is what is within you. Nobody can search for happiness from outside of themselves.

Humanoids are very happy beings. When we were young, we were in our space craft, and we could not live like the others in our own planet. We did not have relationships or the kind of food that would bring us joy. What we ate was always the same Tali food. It is very healthy, and it keeps us in good shape, but it does not taste or look good. Our bodies are very strong and healthy. We live in this craft, and we continue to be very independent. We are very happy. Nowadays, we can bring our wives and live here with a small family. We are happy because we are happy. Not because our wives are here, some of us do not have a wife here and yet they are still happy. If you want to become happy, you must find the happiness from within you. If you are happy and you take a wife or a husband, they will become happy as well.

When you do not wish anything good for others and you only wish good for yourselves, that is the reason why you cannot be happy. When you want to find someone who will love you for who you are instead of your finances or appearance, learn how to be patient and maybe you can meet someone like that.

The old man who had decided to go with the angel now arrived in Heaven. He was wondering about the bodies that were beautiful like the living had, but brighter and more translucent, more beautifully structured, he wanted to become one of them. He asked the angel if he also could have a body like that and the angel said, "But of course everyone in Heaven has a body like that, including you." The old man looked at his body in awe and he could not believe it was true. He could have doubted but he had finally realized that he died. When he had met all the others and he was ready for Heaven, the angel came to him and said, "Now nothing will prevent you from being happy." The man stared at the angel and said, "Dear angel, now that I have died and gone to heaven, can I please go back to Earth where my casket is?"

A-A-A

Children of the Earth, we do not think like you do. Many things are different here. We also cook and live an ordinary life. When we do not want things like sex or an ordinary life any longer, we begin enlightenment. When we want to become enlightened, we do not have sex anymore because it takes the mind away from balance and harmony. We usually begin enlightenment when we have grown old enough and we no longer want to live a regular life. After we have lived an ordinary life for long enough, unlike you, we do not care about such things anymore. Unfortunately, you never get enough of everything that you can do and experience during your lives. We live like we want to until we have lived long enough, then we will acquire enlightenment. What this means is that we will begin to perfect our spiritual qualities.

Eventually, we will leave to meet with Men that will teach us how to become a part of the eternal light. This is how we will continue to be happy when we are old. When we leave to go to these Men we leave everything behind. In a way, we are preparing for an approaching death. We usually leave during daylight and when it becomes dark, we will arrive at a small village where we are expected. When we have not been there during this life, we want to meet all of those who left before us. They have been there for maybe twenty years, and when they want to see their loved ones, they can come and meet them. They want to know that everyone is happy without them, now that they have become old. When we begin telepathy, we can be in telepathy with our families, and in this way we know how everything is.

We read an article about a man who wanted to become enlightened. First, he left and nothing happened, but once he became enlightened, he started to work with people to be able to help them. But the truth is, after you have been enlightened you no longer want to be around anyone else. All you want to do is to be in the spirit God has created. After you have received enlightenment, you no longer want to be around others. If you think that you have achieved enlightenment, then most likely you have not. When it happens, everyone around you will know and will leave because the brightness that radiates from enlightenment is something that nobody without it can bare, not even one of our own. After you die, you will meet enlightened spirit beings. You cannot approach them unless you yourself have been enlightened. When the time comes full, everyone must be ready for anything to happen.

Humanoids do not think that we are a spirit or a body. We think that we are the kind of beings whose spirit lives in a body, and when the time comes, we will leave our body behind. When a human being comes to the end of their road, they think that everything is over. Where is your spirit? What is in the beginning, so it must be in the end. When you want to complete all tests on The Path of the Four Fires, you will realize that there is no escape knowing who you are. When you come to this little planet called Earth, together you will have to go. This means that everyone you have been in contact with will be in a place where you will be judged in accordance with your actions. If you were not stupid and did not cause harm to anyone, then you will be in a good place. However, each one who has inflicted pain on another will have judgment. Everyone who has left before you will be waiting for you to be ready because you owe a payment for what you have done. When you have paid for what you have done, do not complain anymore because from what you owe, you must pay. When you owe someone and you want to forget, the more you try to forget the more aware you will become.

Everyone who wants to forget the evil that they have done has helped Satan. That is why they want to forget, so that they do not have to realize what it was that forced them to do the evil in the first place. When you have done an evil deed for Satan, he will come to get his own. He will find each one that has served him, and he is searching for them, like we search for our own. When Satan comes there is no escape. He will come and say that you belong to him, and if you do not follow him in that moment, you will have nowhere else to go. All roads are blocked when you are Satan's own. When you become Satan's own, you can no longer meet your loved ones, you can no longer be anything other than one of Satan's evil spirits. Some will be in outer space like we are. They will have to obey evil telepathy. They will also have to kill and torture their victims. They are no longer human. They go when Satan says go. They have no will of their own. They are just slaves.

When our own has been on Earth and they have come to the light, they will come back to us and continue life here like we do. They can remember all the lives they have lived on Earth. If they want, they can begin to help those spirits in which they knew, and whoever else wants help developing spiritually. When they come home to their own, they will be as strong as those who have defeated Satan. Humanoids have nothing to do with Satan, but humans need help from someone who has defeated Satan.

You can be just as much like The Sons of Heaven, or you can be like The Children of Satan.

You cannot be both at the same time. You are either like the Children of Satan, or you are like we are. You only have two choices.

Humanoids have come to you so that you will not play with fire.

Why do you want to play with fire?

When you cast spells to get a man or a woman, when you cast spells to get revenge, and when you cast spells to have luck and money, then remember, there is no such spell that would be from God. When God Is, He Is. He is also Great, and when His light touches your spell, the spell comes back to you. Do not wonder what is going on when everything you have done to another quickly comes back to you. When you have cast a spell, you cannot undo it. When you cast these love spells that seem to be quite effective, be careful of what might follow. Some have gone crazy because of love from Satan. It has also killed the people casting the spell if the spell even goes to the right person. When through Satan you want love, it will also be hate. Nobody can ask for love from Satan. When you want good fortune and cast spells, your good fortune can become satanic. What kind of happiness do you think you can ask from Satan? Maybe the kind where if you became happy, someone else will become unhappy, and that the money you receive brings suffering with it. When you want to cast spells to became famous, maybe that fame will be something completely different than what you had in mind. Maybe you will kill someone and that will be your fame. When you cast spells wanting good, do not be stupid, you cannot wish anything good from Satan who is evil himself. When you want evil for him, you will get it, but not in the way you want it, but the way he wants it.

When you begin to repent, in order to make a complete change to become better and when you want to change, do not come and say, "This is not what I deserve." What you get is what you deserve.

Humanoids have always been here monitoring you. Many of you have been here from the beginning. Many of you have even met us. There are women who had wished they could be with us; crazy is the one who would not want to be with us. We do not want to have children with you. When we have children, we take good care of them. We are not like you are and have children and then not love them. When we have a child, we take good care of them. We do not leave them alone in the dark where there are evil spirits. Children are sensitive and they can even see them. When you leave your children alone, Satan can come and try to take them, they are unable to defend themselves. Children do not know how to fight against Satan. If this has happened, provided that you can begin by blessing the child, pray and have the child go through a spiritual cleansing with someone who knows how to do that. If the child cannot be in peace, and there is nobody who can calm the child, and the child is not sick, this could have happened.

So, do not leave your children alone, keep them away from the kind of people who can hurt them. Also, be careful with grown men who only want to be with children. Watch for those who think that children are witless. Babies can be in great danger. Crazy people can take them to be sold somewhere.

Crazy is the one who does evil to a baby. Babies are still with angels, and what you have done to a baby, you have also done to an angel. What you have done to an angel, you have also done to one of God's own. What you have done to God's own will not be forgiven. When you want forgiveness, it will not be granted, no matter how much you try. Provided that you do not want to end up with Satan and you want to repent, first, you will have to go to Hell, and from Hell you still must ask for mercy. When you have been given mercy, you will have to live through karma the same destiny that you have caused the baby. Humanoids do not want to explain how.

The old man finally came to repentance and wanted out of his grave once and for all. When it happened, he never again wanted anyone to come and say that death is a final state, and that Heaven and Hell does not exist.

A-A-A

We are Sons of the Heaven, humanoids, and we begin,

You, Earth's humans have a lot to learn. Unless you want for the body that you have to be all that you can have as your own, with the help of the body, you have to find your spirit. At the time when you were allowed to come to Earth and begin life, you had to understand that you first had the spirit and then came the body. When you came into life and began to live, you eventually lost what you had when you were born, you did not realize that you can lose the spirit that God gave you. Therefore, you have to understand that when you die, you will start everything from the beginning again. When you reincarnate, you cannot be like you were in your past life. If you are, and you have not learned anything, it means there is no development in you. When spiritual development has stopped, it means that you can lose your spirit.

The spirit is a gift given by God, created by angels. Angels create the spirit and God gives it as a gift to the human. When the spirit is young it is able be in the type of vibrational level where you are for long periods of time. When it gets older it cannot be in you, and the spirit will leave. What this means is that you are in danger of disappearing completely. The spirits of the underworld will take over bodies like that and will bury spirit matter and eventually kill it. Those that are seriously mentally ill and mass murderers who kill and kill without any idea of their own are like that. Logically thinking, nobody like that can have a spirit. The spirit will not allow for the human to be completely insane or allow them not to care about anything anymore.

All along, many who have lived through a difficult life can still think despite the difficulties. They did not become evil. This was because their spirit helped them get through difficult times. The spirit is the one, when coming into life, which always wants to be your own. For the spirit to be your own you must find it. You do not even know that you have a spirit, and the only purpose of this spirit is to be conscious while you are alive.

A-A-A-A

When the spirit is free, the human can also be free. The individual does not have to feel the influence of the lower self anymore. They can be in peace; they do not have to do things that they do not want to do anymore.

What is an evil spirit?

The evil spirit is the low spirit that exits in each human being. Like we have previously explained, Satan created a human, a creature that only had the low spirit. God also created a human, a creature that only had the spirit. They were different and there was nothing to bring them together. God then allowed Satan's low human and His human to be joined together. This is how Earth human came to be. After the Earth's human began to wander reincarnations throughout each life, they had to fight for the sake of the spirit that God gave. God's spirit is light, and Satan's spirit is darkness. When this darkness overcomes humans, they are no longer aware of their actions. When they want to become enlightened, they can no longer have contact with the low spirit and the low spirit must die. Therefore, you cannot be both Satan and God's Children at the same time.

Your children that you do not want to take care of belong to Satan. When you do not want to take care of your children, you cause your children to end up with Satan. Everyone who abandons their children have left them for Satan. When Satan takes your children, you will not have much hope either. You have done a service to evil, which is the worst thing that you can do when you have children.

When you begin to pray, you must make sure that your prayer will go to God. Begin prayer that is in the light. When you pray, you must be able to go to the light. You cannot remain in a state where you only repeat the words, the words are not what leads you to God. You must pray in spirit. The spirit is the light, and you must find the light from within yourselves. When you cannot find your spirit, begin by repeating Amen. Amen like Jesus taught. He said that Amen is what follows after the prayer has been finished. When you repeat the word Amen, you can open up to your spirit. When your spirit has been opened, you can experience the light. When you experience the light you can begin your prayer. After you have said your prayer, you must be pure, you must feel yourself to be pure, and there cannot be any sounds from your body. When your body remains silent you have prayed correctly. When you can be completely quiet, and you do not hear any such thoughts that would disturb your prayer, then you have prayed correctly.

When you come into life, you only have the spirit. When you begin to feel the influence of your parents and start to live, the low spirit comes into you. You only have eight months to live purely. When you begin your life, you have an old mind body that Satan has created that has always been unclean. When Satan created the body, he made it so that it would be a complete opposite of the Kingdom of Heaven. Satan made it so that his subordinates who wanted to help him could tempt humans through this body. When Satan created the body he filled it with all kinds of thoughts, like, he who is not always having intercourse is without love. He who does not always want to be completely honest is intelligent. He who is not selfish is stupid. He who does not care what other people think is different. He who does not start having sex when they are young is abnormal. He who does not care about other people can be happy. He who does not care about what others think of you does not care about anything at all.

When you are able to be different like Men are, then you do not want the light to be gone anymore. When you do not live a regular life anymore, but you want to live your life differently, then begin a change of life. Begin this change by being alone at first and study yourself. Do this in a way that you study yourselves spiritually. Begin by praying a lot and by thinking about who you really are. Think about your body, what does it want and what do you want? When you realize that your body wants different things than you do, you need to start cleansing yourself. Your body only wants to eat, drink, make love, and conquer with its beauty. It is only a small body through which the human is able to interpret themselves. It is not meant for the body to control you, you have to conquer it. You have to be your own body's master. When you have come to know your body, you will have to teach it how to obey you. It cannot be the one who rules. When you have learned to know your body, you also have to learn to know the low spirit. The low spirit is strong, it wants to take over. The low spirit is the way that at first, you do not feel its influence in you. It is always complaining about how nothing is worth anything. It wants everything that you do not have. It demands for you to seek a lot of pleasure for yourself. It only wants you to do what it wants you to do, and it will never be satisfied.

When you are always looking for one-night stands and casual affairs wanting to be happy, your higher self will not prevent what is happening to you, you should not play with fire. When you start playing with fire and sex, you are giving the power to the lower self. It will never be satisfied; it will always want more all the time and will prevent you to have peace unless you continue to search for the type of experiences it wants. When it has taken full control of you, you are no longer yourselves.

A-A-A

Men begin again, we begin now.

Children of Earth, you do not realize what will happen to you when you do not want to think about things, and when you continue like you have from one life to the next, reincarnations will not begin and end eternally as you have thought. At any given moment you might have your last chance. Unless you begin to repent, to change to become better, A you might never be able to come back and perhaps you are not ready to completely disappear.

Subordinates are those who come and take away everyone whose development has ended. Everyone working for Satan are subordinates. They come at night and they want those undeveloped souls to follow them.

The man who had just died had only a little time left when he started to have regrets. He was told that his time had come to an end and that there was not going to be another chance, so he had to leave and go with the subordinates. He would have been ready to go to Heaven, but he did not have the time to take care of his spiritual state, and consequently, he never had the time to take care of his spirituality, and now his time had come to an end. He wanted to have the chance to be able to have time to think about what had happened. He had lived many lives in a way that he had never thought about spiritual things. He just came back to life and he would go to work and would live ordinary life like thousands of others like him. When all his time had been fulfilled, there was nothing he could do. When he died, he had to leave with Satan's subordinates.

These low creatures do not have any development. They only do what Satan commands. These low creatures are the kind that they do not even know that they exist. They do all kinds of evil and create telepathic states where the human is unable to be in his own body or find peace anywhere. They take over the human's body and will use it according to Satan orders. These low creatures are not even evil spirits, they are nightmares that nobody wants to encounter, even if paid money to do so. Their thoughts always consist of the following: although you do not have anything, nothing is worth anything, and although you do not understand anything, you do not have understanding because you are nothing, and although you come from light, you will never be able to go back to the light, even if you want to think, it is too late. These are the kind of thoughts they transmit. When they come, they will take over the low self and the lower self begins to rule. As the low self begins to rule, they will fill it with all kinds of thoughts the human, under normal circumstances, would not think of. As these thoughts begin to take over, they will create all types of desires and these desires begin to rule. The human begins to leave his body and when the body begins to fight back, these low creatures will begin a new dreadful task as they create telepathy between the human and Satan that will contain all the satanic thoughts that will come to the mind from now on. What is worse, these low creatures will take over the entire human body for their own use.

They will begin destruction on each sensory level. Everyone knows of such a person who is imprisoned by their own thoughts and strange actions. Normally they are called schizophrenics. They might be in the light from time to time and suddenly everything will go back to complete chaos. New low creatures will create even more until the human will slip into a state where they are not able to know through their body or through their spirit of what is happening to them. Therefore, it is important that you break down all evil thoughts as they surface. When you have received evil telepathy send it away, the same way as it came. Fire, and only in fire burn those who do not banish these low creatures away. When they are gone the human can freely be himself again. When the low creatures have taken control of you, you must overcome them with your willpower.

You must pray and begin the cleansing that we have mentioned. This cleansing means that you will not be around other people and that you will not be left alone without help. You will need to seek help from a highly spiritually developed person who can pray on behalf of you. Soon you will feel how these dark entities leave you. You will burn in fire if these dark entities do not leave you. This fire is pain, when you feel that these entities do not leave you no matter how much you try to remove them, your body will begin to produce painful mental states. These painful mental states can exist in four different levels, the first level is that you cry, the second is that you are no longer able to do anything, the third is that you isolate yourselves, and the fourth stage is that you feel dreadful mental states or agony.

The cleansing must begin by being alone for a while, even if it is just for one day so that you can begin to feel the influence of these spirits. They will start causing disturbances, they will yell and ridicule you and explain, "What a despicable creature you are." You must defeat these voices; you cannot allow these voices to influence you. After the voices are gone, begin by repeating Amen, and after that, you can begin your prayer. Pray one night and one day and when you begin this, you cannot eat or drink and although you are thirsty you can only drink holy water, the kind of holy water that has been blessed by someone who is highly spiritually developed. When after this you have been purified, you must always remain in promise that you will never again be in contact with these spirits. This is how you can return to normal life. Low spirits come when the human is in a weak condition. Normally, something bad has happened to them and the spirit has vibrated in a way that has made it seem broken. This type of conditions can happen to anyone. This does not mean that the person who is under the control of these low spirits is evil, or less than anyone else.

A body that creates many different types of thoughts can also shatter the spirit. The spirit cannot handle all the information that is being offered. When the spirit does not have the strength to maintain its balance, a paralysis-type condition can occur, making it difficult for the human to speak or move. Some people can become completely blocked, where they are not able to read or do anything else. Evil spirits are different, when an evil spirit possess a human, they want to take over entirely. In a case like this, the person will change completely, both physically and spiritually. They can physically be nice looking and healthy, and they may be complaining to everyone that the body that they carry is not a problem to them, but it is a problem to others. The evil spirits normally explain that the person is ugly.

A-A-A

Evil spirits come when the human is weak both physically and spiritually. It will lower their vibrational level when they have been depressed for a long period of time. When the human is not able to be in the light anymore, or when they are unable to love any longer, their aura's color body becomes gray. Therefore, the evil spirits can go inside. This can be caused by difficulties brought by different kinds of life situations. After the evil spirit goes inside, the human will change. Their entire personality will disappear and will be replaced by someone who is unlike them.

The evil spirit will cause difficult and painful mental conditions, and the person's entire mentality will be different. When the spirit begins to battle against the evil spirit, it causes bad states of rage. It is clear that without help in this situation the human is facing a serious problem. He cannot survive alone from what has happened to him. The evil spirit does not want to leave the body it lives in. It will keep the human in a helpless state where the human himself cannot affect the matter. He will be completely open to everything that he sees or imagines that he hears. He is unable to control anything that is happening to him. He is forced to live in the evil spirit's funeral atmosphere. Often, evil spirits will produce a sense of death and they want to lead the victim to death. They want for the spirit who still resides in the same body to leave and does not disturb their life. If the victim commits suicide, they will become free of the evil spirit, but they will soon realize that they left their own life badly unfinished. This can cause an inability to leave the astral planes. We do not wish to explain more about them.

When a bad spirit has possessed a body, that person will need outside help, someone must help him. The person himself cannot prevent the effects of the evil spirit. He can barely understand what is wrong with him. He will experience everything much worse than what he normally would. He wants to die and can feel the closeness of death near him constantly. When he wants to live a regular life, the evil spirit will prevent him and force him to do things he would not normally do. He feels that nobody loves him because the evil spirit does not have a drop of love in it. The human's own spirit is still present, and his own spirit will feel this, "sense of a funeral," where nobody loves him and that the only thing waiting for him is the grave. When the evil spirit leaves, the victim will suddenly be like a different person. The evil spirit may come and go quite freely. This occurs because the human's own aura can quickly change, and the evil spirit is no longer able step in.

When a human has experienced a lot of pain, the borders of their black hole have reached their peak and his aura has become gray. The evil spirit can come through a tear in the aura that the four different stages of mental pain have created. This tear is not the only place where the evil spirit can come through, if the human has experienced a lot suffering the aura spirit has developed a kind of black hole in itself. It is a state where all suffering has gathered matter created by the experience of the pain. The evil spirit can come through this.

What can you do in this situation then? The future most definitely must be better than the past. The human must be helped to live in better life circumstances so that he can help himself to become happy. As the future is in order, he has to learn how to experience happiness so that the black hole will eventually disappear. The evil spirit can always be cast away, but it will continue to come back unless life circumstances can be corrected. When a human who has a black hole dies, he can help himself by practicing meditations and he can pray and practice higher spiritual things. He can do that after he has died if he is spiritually developed and if he was not able to help himself while he was still alive. Spirit beings will help him as well if he is spiritually developed, but, while he is still alive other people should help him into better life conditions away from the disturbances that his living life has caused.

Storks and angels are the kind that will come to help when the evil spirit has possessed the body. They will help the spirit to have the strength in the battle that has taken place in the body. Often the body will get very sick and it only wants to rest. When all this is over the human will realize what has happened. He will want to begin to help himself, transform his life, and meet different kinds of people who do not want to harm him.

When you know how to decorate your homes, and you know how to work, and you know how to read and write, then why not help people who really need your help. Everyone who is in big trouble with evil spirits need your prayers and your help. When you do not help these people, one day you might be faced with the same destiny, only because you did not have any impact on what was happening around you. Help those whose lives have horrible circumstances.

When you fall in love and start being with your loved one, you do not even know who this spirit is. You will just love blindly; you do not care about anything else. Crazy is the one who does not know who they think they love. Sometimes an evil spirit can create a type of mental state that is similar to love. It can make a person crazy for love. It creates a hypnosis-like state where the victim does not even realize what is going on. He is blind to everything but to the one he imagines loving. When something like this has happened, by the time you realize it, it will be too late. Normally it is when you have children, and it is too late to break up the relationship. Evil spirits will begin their work when the victim is no longer free. That will be the end of cheap love. He will soon realize that he has been betrayed, she whom he believed he loved is someone who does not even care about him as a friend. Normally, the evil spirit will choose the type of people who do not love each other in the light. When everything is too late, there will only be difficult life situations and suffering. Many have had to experience this kind of fate. Normally, the evil spirit will not leave this person through which it has influenced. It continues to want to disturb the lives of these lovers. The evil spirit may even cause such that the lovers want to kill each other in the end. They begin to seek things that would destroy them. They want to be free but are unable to do so. Provided that the evil spirit will suddenly leave them, they will no longer want to continue the relationship, and when they separate, they do not want to see each other. This differs from the lovers we have previously mentioned because they do have the courage to see each other when they do not want to. The ones that are joined by an evil spirit are too afraid to even see each other, in the end they will understand that something was badly wrong. When you are not sure of what has happened to you, you can begin with the cleansing method we have above explained. During that process it should be revealed if an evil spirit has brought you together. All that which you will feel is disgust which will stay with you after the spiritual cleansing. If you still cannot be sure, begin by praying each time you meet this person and put holy water on you. When you meet them, the state of pain (strong feeling of nonphysical pain: experience of mental and spiritual pain) will grow so powerful that you will know what you feel is not love.

If you still do not know what is happening to you, think carefully about what happened when you met. When you first began to have the influence of the evil spirit you felt yourselves filthy. This feeling of filth will not go away until the evil spirit is gone. When someone is possessed by an evil spirit who does not want help and continues to come back to you repeatedly, you must pray powerfully each time. Humanoids do not want to explain everything, you can also learn how to think for yourselves.

Human beings that are under the control of the low spirits, evil spirits, lost spirits, or even living spirits must learn the spiritual cleansing method. When the spirits do not leave you, you will need to perform the spiritual cleansing as often as you can until these spirits do leave you. Those with spirits who do not want to get help might not be helped. You can try to explain to them what might be wrong, but if they do not want help, there is nothing more you can do. Like we have above explained, everyone has to learn to understand things on their own. Everyone must want to make amends to become better on their own. The ones who threaten to kill themselves may also be able to kill someone else and that is the impact of the evil spirit. That is why you must know what is going on so that you can protect your own life.

When you want help and cannot find it, begin the spiritual cleansing. You can ask the priest from your congregation to bless the water. When the water is blessed in the church, the water becomes holy because in the church there are many spirit beings who will help the priest purify the water. It will be purified akin to God's Spirit sliding over the water. That is why water is important in all things involving the spirit world. Water is very close to God, Who made all energy with the help of water. Also, a human being's body is mainly made of water. When holy water goes through the body it makes the vibrational frequency higher. This will help the spirit become stronger.

A-A-A

Children of Earth, if you do not want to become like the Children of Heaven, you will become like the Children of Satan. Satan's Children are the kind that they do not want anything good, and neither anything for another. They want everything for themselves, and nobody can be happy. Satan's promise is that you will get everything you want. He has promised love, happiness, beauty, and money, but what kind are these promises? When he promises love, it will be disgusting lust that will help you meet someone whose body is in such a state that it wants to be in the space with you whose body is willing to have sex but they can never love you and they only want to harm you. When you no longer have a body and are still seeking sexual satisfaction, how can you satisfy yourselves without a body? And when you try to take over someone else's body who is still alive, you will become Satan's own. It is important that what you do with your sex life, you do it with love, not with lust. After the lust is gone, you might not even want to see the person who you spend a lot of time with. Why do you waste precious time in life and leave men you could love only because you want sexual experiences with those you do not even like?

When men are constantly searching for one-night stands, they do not realize that they are losing their ability to love. When a man does not love the woman, he wants to sleep with, he has taken Satan's thoughts to himself. Satan wants for human beings only to make love without love. He wants for the human being to lose their ability to love anyone. When you have lost the ability to love anyone anymore, it would be best for you to begin with a thought that unless you want to love truly, you do not want to be with anyone. And when you are alone and are waiting to love someone, then from your own will, you will begin to love. This means that the love in you begins to live again. After you have awoken this feeling you can start dating someone you like. When you do not want to sleep with them, then wait, maybe soon will come a moment that will make it happen. It is important to first get to know the person who you love, after you get to know them you can begin an intimate relationship. After the relationship has begun you should be able leave them and then return to them. What this means is that if the relationship is right it will not end even if you leave and when you do come back everything is as it used to be. In a satanic relationship, as soon as you leave your partner alone, they will be looking for someone new. You can never be in peace in a relationship like that, you can never be sure what they really feel about you. When you can meet without making love each time you are together, then you have also found a good friend. Although we have previously explained that friendship and love relationships are different, what we meant is that normally friends do not want to date each other. When friendship turns into love, normally it has just grown into it. When you do not want to be alone anymore and want to find someone to love, begin praying for God to send you a helper who will bring you the person who is right for you. If you have been waiting for too long, it may be that you have had opportunities that were not as you had hoped them to be, or something had prevented you from staying free. This happens sometimes because there is someone who you are waiting for, although you are not conscious of it on a physical level. When you begin this new relationship, begin it as if you have met them for the very first time, even if they were your old companion from previous reincarnations. Everyone who comes back to Earth must, in each reincarnation, find themselves again. Their telepathy might be the kind that you will, through your body, know what they think. The body normally produces the same telepathy that it has produced in all reincarnations and this old memory can open up and you will end up having the same kind of relationship you did in your previous lives. However, because everything has to change, the body, the spirit and the astral plane, you must be like you would be starting everything for the first time, otherwise this relationship is not able to grow and develop which is the purpose of everything, even in the relationships that begun many lifetimes ago. If you are unable to change this old familiar pattern, it may be that this relationship will end the same way as it did in previous lives. If it does not end, it might not develop and it might end permanently in this life because all spirits that want to develop want to choose the kind of companion through whom they can evolve. When the relationship does not help you develop, then unfortunately you have made the wrong choice, some relationships stop all spiritual development.

What this means is that you will both begin to be in your dreams together, when you are together in your dreams the other one cannot develop during the dream anymore. During your dreams you are together, and you no longer want to learn anything. It is important to want to learn new things. At one time it was the most important thing. When the spiritual development remains at the same level and nothing new is manifesting, this will be like any other relationship without joy. When a human being wants to learn and develop, this means that everything needs to change a little bit all the time. What does not change does not grow, and what does not grow, dies and what dies, no longer exists.

When Satan promised that you can have beauty, he gives you the kind of beauty that you cannot be alone, yet nobody will love you. You will always find company, but none of them will love you, they only want to play through your body. When you are in a relationship where you are not loved, you can feel it. You will always be very lonely, and nothing can take away this loneliness. After you have made love, you feel that you are alone. You will not have a feeling that you were together with someone in an experience that you can share. After the beauty given by Satan has faded, you will have nothing left. Nobody will care about you and you will be very unhappy and lonely when you get old.

When Satan promised fame and fortune, you might get it, but the sacrifice that you must pay for it might be a price that you are not willing to pay. Maybe you will get fame and fortune that otherwise was not meant for you, however, the body is unable to live under circumstances it was not born for. The body wants to be compensated for the life it did not have. The body will begin to misbehave, you might get different telepathy from your body who is saying, "I don't want this life, I want to live a different living life." and consequently you will have to fight against your own body. When the spirit does not interfere because the spirit only wants spiritual development, the body will start a rebellion and you will not know how to fight against it. Provided that you do not understand, be careful, what you do not understand, is what you should understand.

The body can take over by eating, you will start eating such large amounts that you will gain weight. This body that rebels has reached a point where it does not want to live with your decision. When the body is born, it will also be given a promise, if you break this promise, the body will begin to rebel. If you have chosen one of Satan's promises, that is one of those things that the body does not agree with, because the spirit has promised to the body that it can live in peace. When the spirit has broken its promise, the body will begin to rebel, when the spirit has chosen one of Satan's promises, first, the body will get very ill, it becomes ill in a very short time because all the low creatures will come and take over the body. Low creatures begin to manipulate the body and the body does not like this, because now the body must surrender and obey the commands of different kinds of spirits. The body wants to eat, drink, and make love so that it can resist the urges of the low spirits. The low spirits do not care about eating or drinking, they want to make the human do things with the help of their body. Their motivations are different.

Provided that you want to know, in a way, the body is independent as well. In a sense it is an animal that you are meant to take care of, this animal is not the kind you think it is. It knows independently how to be what it is. Mainly it wants to rest and eat, it does not want to be cold, it does not want to have pain, and it wants to be kept healthy. If you do not love this animal, it will become so sad that it does not want to live with you anymore. When it does not want to live with you anymore, it will begin rebellion. In a way, with this rebellion, it wants to push you away. You must love your own body properly. It was born to serve you and it was born to help you so that you may fulfill yourselves.

When Satan promised fame and fortune, this fame and fortune has no blessing, it is the kind that will only cause suffering, not joy. Many people have the kind of karma that will make them rich and famous. This is good karma. When karma like this is fulfilled, it will make these people happy, normally they will do a lot of work for the sake of mankind, and typically they have a higher consciousness. Although life cannot always be harmonious and happy, even if you are spiritually developed and have made all your choices correctly, you do not need to worry. Everything that you deserve, you will get. If you deserve a lot of happiness, you will get it, but if not, then you have not deserved it. Still, you need to do the best you can to do everything right, even if you feel like you are not getting what you think you deserve, perhaps this living life is the last one where you can pay off the rest of your karma, and because of that you cannot be happy. The purpose of life is not to be happy. Although you have a lot of problems, you can find spiritual life and through that you can find happiness that is unlike any worldly pleasures. The low creatures explain that you cannot be happy without worldly pleasures. They will do all that they can to convince to you abandon your spiritual development.

The dead, who are wandering everywhere and whom lack all spiritual development, are always searching for new opportunities to come back to life, a living body is an opportunity like that. They will try to take over a living body and drive away the spirit who lives in it. They are not evil spirits, they are just restless spirits who do not know much about anything. Normally, it is easier for them to take over a body when it is drunk. When the body is drunk it is no longer in cooperation with the spirit, it will release the spirit and it continues to exist in its own animal world. An evil spirit is often responsible when the drunken state becomes very bad very quickly and the human goes crazy. The evil spirits as well take over a body that is drunk. When the restless spirit possesses the body, the body does not care about what happens, because it is no longer in contact with the spirit who lives in it. After the restless spirit has taken over the drunken person, that person begins to behave strangely. They might want things they normally would not want. They might eat foods that they normally would not eat, and they will start talking about things they will not recall. Normally, after the person sobers up, the spirit will go away. When the person who was drunk does not even want to think about what had happened while drunk, it might be because of the restless spirit that was in the body.

When you want to celebrate and drink, remember to drink only so much that you know you are in contact with your spirit. Do not drink so much that that the spirit is no longer in contact with you. You can live, love, and eat normally, although, you want to develop spiritually. You just need to learn how to control yourselves. You need to learn to know who you are now that you have a high spirit and body, and a low spirit.

When you do not want the body that you have, the body will develop all types of problems because when the body knows that you do not want to live in it, it might start to rebel. The body has the same right to live as you have, it has the same right to be loved as you do. As a spirit, you can demand God's love just like your body can demand love from you. This means that you must take care of your body properly. You cannot torture it, and you cannot cause harm to it. You must learn how to love it right and take care of it. The body has its own laws. It can eat without ever getting satisfied. It can drink, never having enough, and it can make love without resting. The body wants many other things as well, it loves everything that gives it pleasure. When other people flatter it, it wants to become more beautiful. When it gets to be the center of attention, it will be happy. When it becomes tired, it can sleep anywhere. If your body takes control over you, then you will become its slave. It will force you to eat, drink, make love and it wants everything that brings it pleasure. When something like this has happened, you must take power away from it. You must begin to grow your spiritual life so that your spirit can become stronger and take the power back to itself. The body itself is not evil so to speak, it is just an animal that has been created to obey the spirit world. The history of the body's evolution is as long as the history of human beings. When God created the human, He gave it a body.

The Sons of God have important information for human beings, we do not want you to only drive Satan away from your lives, we also want you to learn how to live in such a plane where you can control the laws of life and the spirit world. When you were apes, you did not have much telepathy or knowledge. When you were cavemen, you did not know how to read or write. When you are a human being, who has all the opportunities, you must develop even further. No development will ever end, nothing will even begin, unless you yourselves wanted it.

When you began your living life, you wanted to come here. When you came here, you wanted to become better. When you are given another opportunity, make it better. The body does not want to become better. It does not care about things like that. If your body rules your life, then you do not care to develop either because your body says, "I don't care about things like that" and you believe your own body. When the body dies, it can no longer be alive. If you still believe you are your own body, a terrible destiny is waiting for you. When you die you will stay inside your body, not knowing how to come out of your body. After death has taken your body, you no longer know what you are. You will try to stay in this body that is slowly rotting away. You will have to watch it deteriorate and you do not know what is on fire. This is a hell that you have chosen for yourselves. Often, family members come to a grave like this, knowing that someone is still there. Some will even try to speak to you, and even though you can understand that someone is speaking to you, you cannot speak. Why can't you go and meet with those that you still know? This will not happen to animals because they do not have a higher consciousness. They automatically leave their dead body. In a sense, a human being who has a higher consciousness, when spiritually undeveloped, is below an animal. This is how a human being has become the low human that Satan created.

So, the human being that was created by both God and Satan, during their life, can decide where they end up going to in the end. The battle that involves the spirit world is tough, and life can be very difficult, however, many have fought this battle never knowing what happened. Because time has come to an end, it is time for many to find out what has happened. Many have realized this all by themselves, and everyone who comes to Earth has this knowledge in their own spirit.

If spiritual development goes as it should, all information will be revealed through your own spirit. This is not the type of telepathy that some psychic would get, normally, such people are just sensitive to the planes of the astral body and will receive the information from the spirit worlds, higher beings, or lower beings. As we have explained, we do not explain the future, you cannot predict the future through us. We can still explain people's reincarnations and spiritual development. We can interpret dreams and we can help you find peace from your own spirit. Although everyone has karma, and in a sense, everyone has a future, this future can change dramatically, provided you change. Everything that does happen to you, you have the right to influence the outcome with your own choices. Nobody can come to you and explain what will happen to you. When someone does, maybe you will manifest the future that you were told, or perhaps, what should have happened to you will not happen because when the time comes you did not want it to happen, and you will prevent it so that you can control your own life. So, do not go searching for answers for the future from someone who has contact to these low creatures or evil spirits. They can destroy your future by explaining things to you that they never should have explained. When you are searching for answers, go to places that have many spiritual thoughts, but you cannot know who is who until it's too late and when it's too late you can no longer undo that which was done, that is why it is more important to be careful than careless.

A-A-A

We begin.

Children of the Earth, what is a world that has always had the truth? This is a thought that that did not exist before the light. Only the light, the night has always been, but not the light. When the light came, it was no longer just the night, and when the night was absent, the truth was revealed. First there was darkness, then came God's light that created brightness and revealed the truth on Earth.

When you lived here and had no light, you did all the things according to your own mind. Then what kind is your mind? It is like an animal that can never have enough. The body is an animal. The mind is a part of the body. The mind is the kind that does think, but its mind-set is constricted. It pulls many thoughts from the lower self. It also wants to be in control. It controls many people.

When the human being dies, the mind no longer works and the spirit that did not develop has to remain in the lower planes. If the spirit cannot develop, it can eventually die. When you leave this world and you have not spiritually developed, it might be that there is no hope for you. When you do not want give control to the spirit, there is no future. Why don't you want to develop spiritually? Why do you want to give control to your body? Why do you want to give control to your mind? Why do you want to give power to your lower self? When you don't want to give the power to your spirit, there is no future.

When God gave you what you should have, He also allowed the darkness to come. When the darkness came, Satan came with it, and you wonder, what is Satan and what is God.

Humanoids started this and wanted for everyone who wants to become their own to be able to start a change in their own lives. When you do not want to know what God and Satan is, then how can you know who you are? If you do not know who you are, then who does? When your life comes to an end, you must know that the body you have used will die. What will you do? You will go on thinking that you will die with it, but when you do not die, and you still exist, what will you do? You will continue trying to live like you were still alive.

Humanoids have effortlessly taken you in body and spirit here into our craft. We started such a campaign that each human we took would learn something. After we had taught them, we lowered them back to the Earth. They did not know what had happened to them. When they were hypnotized and it was revealed to them, they said that we had conducted crazy experiments, and the ones from the lower planes, said that all we wanted was to insert objects into their noses and so on. We do not do things like that. There is no reason currently for us to do experiments, we do not begin telepathy nor do conduct experiments.

The others conduct experiments. There are many different types. Some are Satan's own. Some take human beings into outer space so that they can take them when the world no longer exists here on Earth. We do not take them, nor do we conduct any experiments. When we did take them and wanted to teach them, they did not think about physical things. They only thought about everything new that surrounded them. They saw our crafts and could talk to us telepathically. We taught them why life exists, how the purpose of life is so that human beings can develop spiritually, that God and Satan exist, and that there are those who are on a higher level and those who are on the lower level. When they returned and we were hoping that they would start talking about the things we had taught, they did not say anything like that at all. They said that the only things they remember with their body are experiments that were done to them that made them go crazy. Like we have above explained, some do conduct experiments.

The body has always been able to rule the human being. After returning to Earth, only the body was able to remember what had happened and was able to talk about it. The spirit never reached the part of the brain where it could have explained what we had taught. Also, not to mention, the body wanted to go crazy after our acquaintance so that the spirit would not be able to speak through it. This is because the body had ruled these people for so long. The spirit was unable to take that power away. When we were teaching these people, we put a substance into their body to let it sleep. When the body was asleep, the spirit stepped out and we taught the spirit. When the spirit went back into the body there was no hope that it would have been allowed to tell what it knew.

That is why we do not want to take humans into our crafts anymore. It was just a waste of time. When the others take you, do not think that it was Men. They are not us. Like we have previously explained, there are many different types of crafts in the sky. Some are Satan's own. When you are taken to their crafts, you will not know whether they are good or evil. That is why it is important for you to learn. There are various methods by which you can know who the ones are who wish to establish contact with you. We will not begin contact unless it is a question of someone like Lea, who is one of our own. When we want to establish contact, the person may feel a strong sense of happiness. As they feel this happiness, they may suddenly feel very tired. Always pray when you can. After the prayer has purified you, we can establish contact. If we are in contact with you, when after the prayer you fall asleep, you can be with us during sleep. When you wake up, you will feel good, and you will feel that you have suddenly realized something. With your body, you probably will not remember what happened because the body does not want to know what happens during sleep. The body just sleeps in its own space and if it is very strong in you then you cannot remember anything. When you begin to remember, you will remember that someone came from somewhere and spoke to you, and you are not even sure who this was or if this was real or not, or what you were talking about when you wake up. Maybe you talked about something that you have not ever heard before.

The low self wants when you pray, for you to pray for Satan. When the low self wants you to pray for Satan, and if you do, Satan can come to you during your sleep. When Satan comes to you during your sleep, you will have severe states of fear. You might see all kinds of evil spirits. When Satan comes to you, the evil humanoids can come to you as well. They affect your ability to pray and they make it so that you cannot move your body, speak, or make a sound, and in this you consider yourselves dead. When you cannot breathe properly, you just want to escape. They normally take the type of telepathy from you that reveals things you want to do. When they know, they will send you thoughts that you can do these things. If you do not, they will start to send telepathy that you will have to implement these things to be good. Usually, these are the kind of things that you would not do, and normally they have to do with sex and everything that you would otherwise refuse. The evil humanoids will help you do things that you think about, but do not want to do. When you are under their control, they will normally want you to be faithful to them. They will keep you as slaves that can be used when they are searching for something. They seem rather bodiless although they do have a body. They also know how to live in the astral planes. You cannot always tell who spirits are and who are evil humanoids. Usually, the ones in the light are good and the dark colored are evil.

When someone who has passed on appears, they are normally quite different. They are not always ghosts, they can hold a very strong form of themselves. Humanoids are usually rude if they are evil, however the rude ones are not always evil. Some of the ones that want to help human beings can also be rude, only because humans are afraid of them. They do not like how humans think of their appearance. When you do not know the kind that you are in contact with, you need to purify yourselves so that your vibrational levels can become higher. Once this occurs, the evil ones do not want to keep you as their prey anymore.

We knew a person who was rude and mean. He only wanted bad things for everyone he knew. When this person fell into the hands of the evil humanoids, he was given horrible telepathy and as this telepathy grew even more horrible, he wanted to become good. He began to visit spiritual events. He assumed that his body would have helped with what was wrong with him. We know another person who started telepathy with evil spirits. He received evil telepathy and finally wanted to become good as well. When the telepathy became even stronger, he also went to spiritual events. The body can only learn so much. Their bodies were the ones who ruled. When they were in these spiritual events, they did not learn much with their bodies. They attended these events often. The body thought that since it was there it will help. The body does not know how to think like the spirit does. The spirit thinks in the kind of level, that it can comprehend rather difficult thoughts. The spirit knows that it is a part of God, and that is why it is also on a very high level.

Humanoids will take away the spirit that resides in you as soon as you do not want to keep it. When you begin to feel that you only have a little time left, your spirit has already gone away. When we begin this, that we take your spirit away, it means that the spirit will be sent back to the spirit matter where it originated from. When the spirit has not developed, it will be sent back to where it belongs, and it can no longer be independent. When we must do this, it is because God does not want you to hold the spirit as your own anymore. After the spirit has been taken away, you can continue to live your living life. You will live your living life to its end without the spirit and when you die, you will die away. This type of person is very much like someone who is mentally ill, who does not have much of an idea left. After the spirit has been taken away, the person can repeatedly do the same thing over and over. When the body is alone, it no longer cares to think, it will stop everything that it used to do when the spirit lived in it. It just becomes an animal who no longer knows who it is. When the spirit lives in the body, it provides an idea to the body. Even if the body could be in control, its idea for itself is still the spirit. Although the spirit is not in control, it continues to live in the body. After the body dies and the spirit is free again it can continue to develop even through death. When the spirit returns, it will be a little stronger than it was in the previous life.

A-A-A

We do not want humans to always leave the one that they have loved. If you no longer love this person who you used to love, you cannot just leave them and say, "it's all over". When the love has suddenly stopped and there are no feelings left, you can pray to be able to feel love towards this person again. When you no longer want to continue the relationship that does not bring you joy, you cannot go and leave this person who used to be so important to you. When you have created a relationship, you must take responsibility for this person. When they are ready to end the relationship as well, then together you can decide things in the future. When the love stops suddenly and you do not know what you should do, read the part from the New Testament about being united in love. If your feeling was not as it should have been, maybe you never loved. This feeling that was in you came from somewhere else. Now that it is gone, you no longer want to continue the relationship. When you are ready to end the relationship but the other one still wants to continue, you must be responsible for your choices. You cannot play with people. When you play with people, you are playing Satan's games. When you play Satan's games, you are his own. When you want to have friends and you do not want to be alone, then make a friend and wait until love comes into your life. When you grow old and there are not many people who you had loved during your lifetime, then you will know that you have made wrong choices. When you have made wrong choices then you know you are part of the little game that Satan has designed for you.

When you made wrong choices did you not know what you were doing? You were not close to God. One that has distanced himself from God will make many mistakes that cannot be corrected. When you are old and cannot correct anything anymore, and nobody wants your body, or your beauty, you will finally realize what love is and what it is not. When you can no longer find anyone who cares about you, then you will know that it is God's intention so that you may learn something. When you must learn, you will be taught, and when God wants to teach you, He also loves you, and when He loves you, you are in a lucky position. You still have hope, and maybe soon you will get what belongs to you. When you no longer want to live and feel lonely and disappointed about everything in your life, you have to start everything all over. While you are still alive, if you are not excited about anything anymore, search for new things. You can start to grow the spiritual part of yourselves. You can even try to practice spiritual cleansings that will bring you closer to God. In this way, you can find new things in your lives.

Humanoids have been here near you Children of the Earth for a long time. We come when you call for us. When you want, we will help from our space craft. We brought a man into our space craft when his only wish was to be in our space craft. When he finished praying, he would always ask that we contact him and that he could meet with us. He was quite a lonely man, and he was not able to enjoy his life. When he was finally able to meet us, his way of thinking changed. He realized what the purpose of life was, that the only purpose of life could not be meeting humanoids. Men live their own lives as well. He realized that we do work and live like humans, but our lives are much happier because we do not want to harm each other. Spiritually, he wanted to grow and learn how to live the right way. He also wanted to learn to love another person right. He had lived alone, isolated from others although he could have made someone happy for himself. Humanoids will help you, but we do not want you to ask for help just so that you can tell everyone that humanoids helped you. However, you may say that we did help.

The body has always come first in your minds. The body wants to be different and better than others, that is why you have so many complexes. When you do not live in spirit, and you live through the body, and when the body wants help, we cannot help it, because it is under the laws of the body where we live under the laws of the spirit. When we offer help, it is only spiritual, and the spirit will never want to brag and say, "I received help from the humanoids." Men have also taken a woman into our space craft. This woman wanted to be able to meet men who did not want to harm women. After meeting with us, she could no longer be with the men she met on Earth. She wanted someone for herself, but she could not find anyone who did not hurt her. In her case, we helped her in a way where she developed a healthier sense of self and she was able to meet a man who loved her and did not want to wound her. Humanoids do not normally do this, we do not take humans into our crafts.

We look like aura colors. Your prayers have reached us, we know that you want to know who others are and who Men are. When Men started to live near you your prayers became even stronger. Who are Men? Which ones are bodiless? Who are the Others? Humanoids have a body like you do. Our bodies are just much finer in material substance, not such as yours. Our men's body is not quite like your men's bodies are. Human bodies are in bad lust all the time. Women can have intercourse with everyone. Your men are too afraid to love, they would rather have sexual relationships. You have a man's world. Your women are not given any value. The only women whose position is better are those who take care of small children and others who need care. When a woman does not want to take care of small children and wants to be single, people think that she is strange. When a woman does not care about women's role, she is made to be a lover. When a woman wants to be intelligent and also wants to have love, men are too afraid to love her. In your society, the man's role is better because they live through their bodies. That is why their spiritual development is very poor. Men rule your world although they do not even know how to love. Humanoid's way of thinking is very different than yours.

When you want to no longer sacrifice your children, or your loved ones to Satan, you will realize that Men have been in your thought patterns, and we know what you do. When you cannot trust your prayers anymore, begin a spiritual cleansing. Maybe your lower self has been the one who has controlled you for too long. Humanoids created this telepathy so that you can understand what this life is. Many are here for their last time. The time is beginning to be full.

The symbol of humanoids is the stork, who symbolizes the new coming when the time is full. The stork has always been the symbol of birth, the bird that brings the baby. When the time has come full, and the child is ready to be born, the storks will come. We come because it is time.

When you have been waiting and you still wait, when you no longer have the strength to search for answers to all the questions, like we have explained in the beginning, after this, Men will not begin this contact again. Our paths have united once again, like our paths united in the beginning, so they will in the end. Humanoids do not want telepathy from a body who does not have a spirit, there are many amongst you living without a spirit, and if the spirit is that weak, we do not want to meet with it. Humanoids created this telepathy through Lea's spirit. Her spirit was very strong after surviving all her funerals, all the curses and Satan. Then, she was ready for this. When you have done the same, we might think about contact like this, but as you now know, it is not that easy to receive telepathy from Men. Satan's telepathy is easy to receive, it comes very easily.

A-A-A

Men begin.

Children of the Earth, there is only a little time left. Unless you want to end up belonging to Satan, make a change now to amend and become better. When you do not care, and when you do not want to think, there are so many who don't want to think. Why don't you want to think? Maybe it would help you to realize what is going on on Earth. When you do not think, you do not know who you serve, and you do not know who is driving you to do the things that you do not want to do. Humanoids have been away from here for a long time. We were not always here. We came here after everything had gone chaotic. We came back to you so that you could have an opportunity. Even just one opportunity before everything is over.

We are here as the form of I.

We are here as individuals,

we are here like you are.

We will begin the work that will help you.

We are as humans amongst you. We are like one of you and we come as humanoids when we have to. We do not ever think bad about humanoids like humans do. When you meet us, we talk about them like they would be as ordinary as you are. When you meet us, we will help you. We will also help you to realize things. When you meet with us, you do not know who is who. We come in as humans and nobody knows who comes towards them. It is very difficult for us to like you. We are not like Jesus was. He loved you like God loves you. We are our own selves. When you are so close to Satan, when you are so strongly controlled by your own bodies, when your mind is too strong, when you do not want to think about anything, and when you are in telepathy with Satan, then we cannot love you. We feel disgust towards you, yet we do not show it. You will never realize when you have met us.

When we come, and as we begin our work with you, you will not know who we are. When we leave, you will not know who this was who you got along so well with. After you can no longer find us from the four different cardinal directions, then you will know that you have worked with us. Humanoids will come and leave in a way that you will never find us. When we come, you yourselves will change. Later you will realize that you are not who you were before, and when you cannot meet us anymore you will always stay waiting until you can meet us again, but maybe you never will. That is why you should not be involved in Satan's work. If you meet us and you work for Satan, everything that you do or think about us will burn in fire. Everything that you do to us, you will do to God's own, and everything that you do to God's own is something that you will not be able to survive from. When you do evil, and you do it to your own, who are also Satan's own, then your evil is not as bad as the evil you do to God's own.

Why don't you start the spiritual cleansing? Why don't you want to learn to love? Why don't you want to learn to think? You are not animals or any spirits of the low world. You still come to God and you still become clean after burning in hell's fire. Why don't you want to be happy and why don't you want to not have to go to Hell anymore? When you do not know how to think, you do a lot of evil that you do not even realize you have done. When you serve Satan in this way, it is just like any other evil. It does not make you pure when you say you that you did not know what you were doing and that you meant no harm. You just do not want to be responsible for being mean, and you do not want to take responsibility for being evil.

A-A-A

Men begin.

Children of the Earth, provided that you live like you tend to live, nothing turns so white as the wall that was dirtier than the other walls when it was cleansed. When the thick dirt covered the wall, the surface of the clean wall underneath, in a sense, was protected. When you do not begin the cleansing, then maybe you can never find what is pure in you.

Humanoids intended to come and speak to you, but you do not want to become pure. To be able to receive what we have to say, you have to be pure. When you begin to change your life, you must change your whole way of life. You cannot have other people in your lives just to take advantage of them. It is not enough to become better, that you help other people. The body begins that work. Crazy is the one who does not understand what the truth is. This is why your time is soon over and done with. To become better you must become pure.

The Stork is the truth.

When you realize that you have never loved anyone, you will realize an important thing. Your love has been wrong, you have never learned to love. When you have not learned to love, you might never learn to love. When you do not get another chance, you will not have a part in love. When you no longer have a part in love, you cannot be a part of God. When you are not a part of God, you are part of Satan.

Satan does not love anyone. He does not care, nor does he want to know anything about love. His only work is to drive humans away from love. When he has done the work that he must do, he promises you a future that you do not want to give up. This future is the kind that you will never want to love again. The ones in Hell are those that take what he promises, temporary affairs and different kinds of sexual experiences. The body does not fight, it does what it has to do. The body can be one with either man or woman, the body does not fight but the spirit cannot join to a man or a woman's body the same way. The spirit only wants someone who is like it is to be able to be in harmony. When we talk about love, we do not mean that love between a man and a woman would always be love. The only true love is love towards all living things and all that God has created. Everything that God has created, you want to protect and care with love. When you choose from two, always choose the one that is closest to God. When you want to make the right choices, make the one that will help you develop spiritually.

When you do not want to serve Satan anymore, you have to let go of everything that is satanic. When you can live without any love from another person, you have found God's light. When you meet people that need help, help them. You do not have to go anywhere searching for someone to help. When everyone has been given someone who they need to help, when you have done what you need to do, your soul will be clean. Humanoids have spoken about the future. When you come to a time where there is no more future, you will realize that everything that has been predicted is within yourselves. You will realize that what was kept in secret was the future. This future that is hidden within you will be revealed. You will be able to see things that will happen. You will be very clairvoyant because of your time is beginning to end. When you reach this point, you must be very careful. The Storks are closer than ever before. When we create telepathy and we explain to you what will happen to you when you do not want to change, and when you do not want to change there is no more future. Provided that you do not care, you are not Children of God but Satan's own.

When you enter a state where you see the future, you will see the suffering of mankind that is worse than ever before. Practice of white witchcraft and practice of black witchcraft is everywhere. The others want good and the others want evil, but you will realize there is no such witchcraft that could have good in it. With the help of evil, you cannot serve good. When you think that you serve God with white magic, you will always serve Satan. For this reason, you need to be careful when the future is suddenly revealed to you. You will realize what will happen to you and what will happen on Earth and when you realize that everything you have seen is here, at this point you can no longer make mistakes but you must know what is happening. When you realize that everything that you saw is true, and when you finally give yourselves as a sacrifice so that God can help others who need help through you, you will know that you have made the right choice. When God begins to lead your lives, people will come into your path who will need your help. God will send these people to you.

When you have chosen Satan, Satan will send you new victims that you must destroy. You will realize that we will not help those who no longer have any hope. Those are the ones that can no longer come close to God. The ones that cannot be in the light anymore, these are the ones that are pure evil. There is no speech or effort that could affect them anymore, they have made their final choice. When you have never been near God, it cannot be easy to find Him. You will more and more often begin to search for God from nature and from the future. Nature is an area created by God, and when you go into nature you will become a part of this area that God has created. This is the reason why you long for nature. In the future God is closer to you. When you search for a connection to God, you must grow worthy of that connection and when you say that you have found God, you will come to realize that God cannot be in you unless you are such matter that He can become a part of you. When you come near God, you will realize that God has helped you to come into life. The future is always in the hands of God. Anyone can give you a prediction, but the only real prediction is the one that God has given to you. What this means is that within yourself will realize what will happen to you. All this is within you. Search and you shall receive. Evolve your spirituality because your spirit wants you to help it grow. Because of this you do not need to know anything about the future as you will realize all this knowledge is within you.

A-A-A

Lea, Men begin.

Men have started to help humans throughout the past few centuries. Although we have not been physically present, we have been aware of what has happened on Earth. We have helped by coming to you in your dreams and by coming to you when you do not have the strength to go on. Maybe you will not remember anything about this, but you will have had a strangely good feeling that you could not find an explanation for in the midst of all your troubles.

When you do not know what life is, then you do not know how to control it. You live like the blind in the dark, you do not know what is happening and why. Humanoids can impact everything else, except evilness. We cannot prevent evil. We are not involved with evil, nor can we change it. It lives under its own laws. When evil has come into your lives, you yourselves must think of what to do. You always must banish the evil from your lives. Jesus was here on Earth, and even He was possessed. Satan tempted Him, and He had to defeit Satan, not even God helped Him. You will always come to this state, between Satan's Earth and Heaven where you must make choices. When you are being tempted you have to overcome it. Humanoids cannot help when you have called for us and whispered, "Please help me when I'm in bad fire." When you are in temptation and you do not know how to help yourselves, you have not passed the test that was given to you so that you can develop spiritually like you should. When you begin to feel strange feelings that you are being tempted spiritually, and that you are being called to join a state where you would become impassive, different than what you normally would be, be extremely careful. Behind this is normally evil humanoids. They know how to use, in a way, a type of hypnosis that is very difficult to wake up from. They take their victims during the night like we would, but they create severe states of fear and sleep like hypnosis from which it is difficult to wake up from. You will also develop problems with your memory. They usually want the victim to leave the Storks whom they are in contact with during sleep. When you do not know what is happening to you and you are in deep trouble, produce the type of telepathy that is meant to drive the evil away.

This type of telepathy is the kind that you will have an impact in everything that you do from spiritual planes as well. You do everything in spirit and strengthen the spirit in meditation. When you go to sleep, place small altars around your bed with holy water, crosses of Jesus and flowers with white pedals. You will make these small altars and pray with them so that you can receive protection from the spirit world. Many good spirits will come to help when they are called. They can establish contact through water and scent. After you have prayed with the cross of Jesus, it will bring good spirits that will guard your sleep. After the evil humanoids have finally left you, you can be sure that the Storks will come back again. When the evil humanoids have already taken control and you cannot become free, you must find a person who can begin the prayer for you.

This is technically exorcism. The evil humanoids are in a way evil spirits, although they are alive. They have a body, and they have their own space crafts. They come during the night like we do, and their astral body is dark. They can become quite visible, and many have seen them. Their work is mainly to try and prevent our connection, and they also want to take parts of the body that they can at some point use for their own purposes. They take tissue and they program the brain to obey demands. They do announcements and transmissions through human brains; they can keep a human as a living transmitter to be in contact with one another. When you come back from their space crafts, you are not the same as others to the humanoids because you have been brainwashed by them. You trust them although they are evil. Your body can become seriously ill and when you get severe mental health issues it is most likely because you have been in their space crafts. When you come back at first, you cannot remember anything, but after hypnosis your memory can return and you can remember everything else, except that you were kept as their slaves who they can even rape or beat among other things that you do not want to remember even in hypnosis.

They hate humans because the humans still have a spirit, they only have the low spirit that Satan created. They are not the ones who were in contact with one well known person (Translators of this text will not reveal the name for legal purposes), these were others, they do not want peace, they only want war. They do not even talk about peace. There are many of us, there are others, and then there are other ones, and there are even the kind that you have not met. Some are young, the ones who speak telepathically have a body. The spirits speak like the living and speak in astral planes. Mediums who can see them can also hear them. Humanoids, almost all the species use telepathy. There are many like we have explained.

Men only come in the type of planes that you can be sure that Men have come. When you think that we are not good, pray that you are not calling the evil ones with your thoughts. When the evil ones come, we cannot drive them away. They can come and go freely according to God's Laws. Some have liberties that others do not. Men do not take you into our crafts like we have said in the beginning. We have done that, but there are only few who have met us. Humanoids have taken some because they were our own or because it helped them. The others come; we are leaving. (We have explained to Lea)

Then came the Others. They are not evil. They study humans and take them into their space crafts. When the Earth will be destroyed, they will gather humans like Noah did at one time in order to save the human and animal race.

They are not human reincarnations; they are their own kind. Normally, they have been refining men from their sperm so that they can also do cross breeding later on. They want for humans to also have their genes so that you can become a little bit better and so that they can work a little closer with humans. When they come to you, you will not remember them either. You do not like them because they are too different. You think they are better than other kinds, but you think that they are strange. They do not like this telepathy, it hurts them. They do not think that humans are strange. They also produce different kinds of telepathy. Usually, the purpose of this telepathy is so that you can learn to love animals and nature. They want you to take care of animals and nature. Men produce telepathy about the spirit and God. And the other kind, of which there are many, establish contact sometimes so that you could learn how to think universally.

Space is so grand and what you can learn in one lifetime is only one small part of what is God's Kingdom. When you are like animals, and you do not want to think and do not want to learn anything, eventually, you have to be removed from the universe. Not even Satan will take the kinds who have not learned through their low selves of what he is trying to teach. It is not enough that you are good or bad. You also must be able to develop. Without spiritual development you will only dry away like old tree branches.

The Path of the Four Fires

A-A-A

Men begin.

Children of the Earth, you come to a time which no longer exists. You will come back to where you came from. When you come back, you will not have a lot of time left, do not rush because of it. When your time is coming to an end, you will understand things. You will see the past and the future. Humanoids have this ability when they are born. We are no longer under the laws of karma, nor do we do evil or are part of Satan's plans. When you come to the point when you realize what is going on, you will trust what we have explained. When your time on Earth has ended, you will meet people that want to help you so that your spiritual development can grow. When you no longer care what these people are teaching you, you have made your choice.

When you begin to live through your low selves, and you become evil, you will also be in telepathy with Satan, who will take care of the rest. When you realize that you can no longer be embodied, and you cannot have another chance, you will often start killing people because you know there is nothing left for you to do. When you start doing evil, you cannot stop, nobody can help you anymore. When you still do not want to stay in this state, you will bury your spirit so it no longer has to suffer because of your choices. When the spirit is gone you are Satan's own.

When you come to this fire where the spirit is dying, you will be in a type of purgatory. During this fire, the spirit dies piece by piece and returns to a place for the ones that have lost hope. It is a state where the spirit returns to the element of what it is made of. You will not feel death, nor will you feel life. When you want to believe that everything you have thought and done will be forgiven, you are greatly mistaken. You are even responsible for each thought. When you do not think of what you do, you will have to live a life that will force your thoughts to move. When you do not care about what has happened because of you, you have to live in a grave of sadness. This is the kind of life where you are not able to enjoy your life, no matter what happens. No matter how many good things happen to you, you cannot feel happiness.

When you learn how to live right, you can be happy also on Earth, regardless, all evil will come through your own decisions. Because of this, you cannot blame God that the world you live in has little joy and a lot of suffering. God did not want you to make the world how it is now, you did it to yourselves.

Lea's life was very difficult as you know. She was not able to enjoy her nice character, or her nice appearance, she was also very intelligent and very talented. Humanoids wanted to help her, but people prevented it. What God gives, humans have taken away. It was not meant to be that her life was as difficult as it was. Many happy things were meant for her as well. When nothing can be changed anymore, those who have prevented her happiness are held responsible. It was through a miracle that she still had the strength to continue her life where the low spirits had taken full control.

Happy things are important in life, humans cannot live without joy. Everyone needs a drop of happiness to be able to continue their life. When the happiness is completely gone, the human does not have the strength go on and they will die one way or another. Like flowers that do not have water. Flowers also need light. Plain water is not enough. When one of the things that the flower needs is absent, the flower will die. When you do not want for anybody who is near you to be happy or joyful, then you yourself must leave. You have been without happiness for too long, and you cannot even handle seeing what others can experience. That is why everything that you do to others, you do to yourselves. When there is an unhappy person near you, they are unhappy because they cannot enjoy the small things in life anymore. When you do not care what they feel, you will become part of their pain, and when you are part of their pain, you will get what you did not want to give to them. Because of this, also learn to love those in whose life there has been no love. Not everything you think is what you know. You do not understand that. What you think is right is not what the truth is. If you love right, you also want to respect another person's will and their different types of feelings. You cannot just love and imagine that you know who the other person is. Humanoids have spoken a lot about love. When each human has their own soulmate, and when they cannot find them, you think that everyone who you fall in love with is your soulmate. You do not even know this person, and you do not even trust your own intelligence when you follow your love. When you do meet your own, who really is your soulmate, you will not doubt anymore. You will change in a way that will enlighten you and it will not cause any trouble. When in some life you are given a chance to meet them, they are not as you think. They are like you are and you then must know yourselves. When you are given the chance to meet your only soulmate, then you have some mission to do on Earth. They will only come to help you so that you can do what you have to do in peace. When you do not fulfill your work, then you will be in the shadow of your own happiness, and you did not fulfill God's will. When you meet them, they are very much like you are, they are not different, but they are as you are. They will help you to become spiritually better than others. When you are together, you will be strong and spiritual, and you will be the kind of person that people will come to in search of light and love. When they are not a part of Satan's plans through their low self, then neither are you. When they are Satan's own, so will you be, but nothing will stop you from coming back to God if two wants that.

Eva was the one who had a soulmate. She was given her own Adam. When Eva fell into sin, Adam had to fall. Also, everything that you do, you also do to your own. (soulmate) Although you cannot meet them in this life, you are the one that can cause harm in their life. When you reach a point where you are allowed to meet them, you must be spiritually awake. If you are not, you can lose them. Without the spirit you cannot recognize them. Their spirit is like your spirit is, and when your spirits become one, they will be in the light without physical meditations. When you want to meet them, you must be ready to let go of yourselves. This means that when you meet them, you are part of them and they are a part of your future life. The ones living on the Path of Four Fires cannot usually meet their own because of Satan. Satan did that for the ones that loved him. He prevented the love that comes from God.

When you have loved Satan, you may never have a chance to meet your own. When you want to meet your own, you just have to pray for mercy from God. When you are unsure if you have met your own spirit lover, then you have not met them. When you get mean remarks, you are not happy, or you cannot be in harmony, they are not who you want. When true couples want to be together…

A-A-A

Men continue.

(Beautiful little Lea does not care about what others explain. Personal for Lea)

A-A-A-A

When real couples want to be together, they are not together so that they can be with someone and not be alone. They are together because they have a future together. They think about the future and they want to be together because they feel good when they finally can meet. Once they meet, they feel that they belong together. Normally it happens immediately and they know that what they feel is something deeper than the current feeling. They trust this feeling and begin to follow it. When they are together, they normally get very happy, and they want to be able to do everything together. They read the kinds of books that they can talk about together, and everything else they do, they want to do together. When they have met, they do not want to separate. They know that there is no one else like the one they have found. In the future, they usually help people and will do a lot of good together. In a way they have a difficult mission to help mankind, and this other one is there to help. When they trust each other as a human would trust in himself, they do not have such problems as jealousy. They cannot doubt one another. Regardless, these relationships are very rare and there are not many that will be given the chance to meet their soulmates. When something like that happens, it is when it is a question of something of great importance.

Short is a human's living life. There is not much that can be achieved during one lifetime. When someone has work that needs to be done, they normally receive help, but the ones that do not receive help are our own. They are very strong and can survive without help, but if someone wants to help them, they will receive blessings for doing so, and all those that try to prevent them will have that returned to them in bad karma.

When you trust and get betrayed, then you must think, who did you trust? You cannot trust just anyone, neither can you doubt everyone. The body is the kind that it does not want to trust the spirit. It doubts the spirit all the time. It repeats that the spirit does not even exist. It wants power, and once it regains power, you are in trouble.

When you are very disappointed in someone, you must think of what kind of people they are, of whom you wanted to trust. You want to trust someone without even knowing them. You will always come to this, "Trust me." As you know, you cannot even trust yourselves. That is why you do not blindly trust anyone, not even those that have said that they are humanoids. You will later realize yourselves what the truth is. When you finally rest, and you can feel all of the things that have been told to you, you will know the truth.

When you meet new people, do not trust them right away. Give yourselves time to get to know them. Provided that they do not want to give you time, forget them. When you trust a person too much, you will only be disappointed. Afterwards, it may be difficult to get over this disappointment. When you approach someone with slight reservation and give yourselves time to get to know them, then you will not get wounded as badly. When you need love, and you cannot find anyone, then be patient. Maybe tomorrow you will meet someone who is suitable for you. When you do not care about who you choose, you can make the biggest mistake of your life. This could be a mistake that you cannot undo.

A-A-A

Children of the Earth, you come to receive telepathy that has always existed here on Earth. When you realize that you live your lives from telepathy, you will realize that you are not who you think you are. When you realize that you live in telepathy, you will notice that men and women will always be like you are. There is no difference in love between a man and a woman, with the exception that men think they have more privileges than women. When you realize that you are nothing more than spirits, and that there is time behind you in which you have not explored, you will realize that you have followed telepathy rather than the spirit, then you will realize what the spirit is.

You only think a little bit. You have large brains, yet you do not know how to use them. You are just as simple as animals who at least have their instincts, if you don't stop this waste of life, you might not get another opportunity.

When you come into life, you are just a spirit that is joined into flesh and bone. In the beginning, the spirit is still as small as a child, and as it grows you will begin to make decisions. You will begin to choose between good and evil. You are given all the information of telepathy. One telepathy comes from God, and the other from Satan. You are the one who chooses. When you do not want to participate in Satan's telepathy, then you cannot make the wrong choice. When you do not always know which choice is the right one, you will need to practice the spiritual cleansing so that you will know. When you do the cleansing, you will know which choice is the right one. When you do not care, you will always do in accordance with Satan's choice. It is very serious when you think that you have always been right. When you think that you have always been right, then you have chosen Satan's telepathy.

God develops humans through mistakes. He allows the human to make mistakes no matter how good he is. For this reason, in love, be a part of God's love. Like He sees things, you must see them. We do not always begin this as you want. When you want us to begin where we have ended, you are mistaken. Who can explain God's Laws other than God Himself.

A human being can not know God's will while closing their eyes and while doing things assuming they are always right.

When a woman asks who has been created for her, nobody can say, "This man that you are with right now is the one who is your own." When God created humans, He created humans so that the human could learn and spiritually grow greater. For that reason, there is nobody who can come and say, "Only this man is the one who can be the one in your life."

When the spirit grows, it wants to change, and when the spirit changes, it can no longer continue doing things as it used to. When the spirit has awakened, it can no longer be in a dream state like it had been, and when its time has come, it must continue its journey. For this reason, do not be stupid and think that what was yesterday will be tomorrow. When the spirit changes, it can no longer continue doing things as it used to. When the spirit has awakened, it can no longer be in a dream state like it was, and when its time has come, it must continue its journey. When today you want to live with someone, maybe tomorrow you no longer want them. That is why you should not live in a way where you will not change. As time exists, so does an opportunity. When an opportunity comes, the Storks will come, and when the time has come full, they will come and choose the ones that are our own. Men also cannot know who is the one we will get first, and who is the one we will take last.

You can develop yourselves to become worthy of who you are. When once again you begin to search for happiness, and you are seeking for new memories, do not play with anything that might destroy you or that person. When you live together, you must also learn to love the ones that you do not love anymore. Love that lasts for a short moment can be the one that will destroy your lives. So be careful when you do not know what you do.

When you seek telepathy from someone who can see the future for money, you must be careful. You cannot know whether that person is in telepathy with Satan or God. When you do not know, then you cannot know what they will explain to you. Maybe they will destroy the happiness that God wanted to give you. When you can not know the future with money, then how can you know the future without it? The future is what you are, and unless you are nothing but the future, then you do not exist either.

When you came here, you came after many hardships. You came here after many difficult reincarnations, and when you can still start over you usually want atonement for those difficult times that you cannot even remember. You will also want a lot of love that you were deprived of because of Satan. When you search for love and cannot find it, you will take anything just so that you can have something. When you take just anything, it also will be just anything and once again you will be without love. In the lowest form, love is not even the body's love. It is a victim of the devil.

When you do not care about what kind of love you have, then you do not know who you serve. You can also start any type of prayer from yourselves, but not all prayers are holy. Even though you think that words are what makes the prayer holy, the prayer must be prayed in spirit for it to be holy. It is the same thing with love. Unless the love is in the spirit, it is not holy. As you realize it is not easy even to trust yourselves. How can you trust someone else? As you will come to know, trust is only in the spirit, not in the body, which will never know what it wants.

When you choose wrong, you have to pay the price for that choice. You cannot trust in anything that the other person says. You can only trust in your own spirit, who is the only one who knows the truth. When you do not know your spirit, you can never know yourselves. Who was funny? Who was beautiful? The one who was in spirit is the one who is. All other thoughts that you will begin to receive is telepathy that is from the spirit and telepathy that is from the brain. When you do not know how to separate telepathy from the spirit and the brain, then you will never know the truth. Many have been badly mistaken when they have trusted telepathy from the brain. These have been thoughts sent by another living person, which on its lowest form, is not better than low telepathy sent by Satan. When the living send telepathy, they usually want to take away the light from the person they send it to, in a way they take away this person's power so they can use it.

This is done by witches, whom you might or might not know.

Sometimes, the witch is not even aware of what they are. They just bother the lives of the other living with their thoughts that they send to the victim, who will suddenly become very tired and depressed. Nowadays, there are many who are completely aware of what they are doing. When you want to get rid of someone like that, then always make the right choice so that with God's help your light is protected. Become more developed, which will make you stronger. The more you live under the Laws of God, the less you live under the laws of Satan. The witches who use others energy are in very low planes. In a way, they cannot live with the help of their own light. That is why they suck the light of others to be able to live a normal life. When you feel that your strength is being taken from you, then ask for God's help, who will then send you protectors so that you can be in peace. When you get mad and crazy from someone's telepathy, then most likely someone is using your energy. Like we have explained, you cannot help yourselves unless you live under God's Laws. We will explain more about these Laws, which are difficult to learn unless you have understood first what we have already explained.

(The end of the 1st journal titled, "The Path of the Four Fires")

We are not claiming that it would always be fun here on our craft. We just think that when the work is finished, we can go back home where we have our family and everyone who we love. However, we want to finish the work in which we started. Humanoids cannot trust the Children of the Earth who will be embodied in the craft of the Storks. Sometimes nowadays, seldom, but sometimes, you can be born and come into our craft as one of Men. We are not saying that it would happen often, but it does happen sometimes. When a child of the Earth is born into the craft where we live, you are not trustworthy. You say that you live like Men and that you want to be like Men. It is sad but true, we can never trust you. You will always be what you are. You create a lot of pain to small beings whom you meet. You kill and threaten so that you can become one of Men. When you are given the opportunity, you will always create a lot of red color to the small planets, which means that you are not good but that you produce pain.

When you can be born among us, this means that you are given a future to learn things that you cannot learn on Earth. When you are given a chance to be born among us, you usually continue to think like you did on Earth. You do not know how to be like Men even in your new environment. Humanoids trust each other, Men trust each other, but the Children of Earth will never learn to trust.

The Children of Earth do not know who is the one who is best, or who will just come to bury their relatives and go like they have come. This means that you never learn to let go of things when the time comes.

Family who you love is not always the kind that you love, but you hold on to them, like you had never even loved them. When you love right, then you also know how to let go. You have to learn to let go of things and people. When the time comes, you have to let go of everything. When you have the time to live and to love, then do so when it is time. When the time is over, it is over, and you have to move on.

Men have our own little families here, some of us, not all, only some are here. Others do not bring those wives who are not needed, because women also do the work that Men do. The wives who we do bring with us also do this same work. They might get pregnant and have children, they do not always know who the child that will be born is. When we know that the child who has been born is a Child of the Earth, we will come and bury him on Earth when he dies. We will trust that he will come back to us when he is ready. Only the ones who want to belong to Men can come back, but many do not want to. Many will want to stay as a Child of the Earth and continue to evolve in their path.

A Child of Earth can be recognized immediately, even as a baby he is not like Men. Provided that a Child of the Earth is born to us, we take good care of him and after he dies, we will come in the name of peace and bury his material remains on Earth. When he is among us, he will learn things and he is usually much more spiritually developed when he is born again on Earth. Usually, they will become great leaders or great scientists, and they can be very intelligent and highly spiritually developed in their next life. When they come back to Earth, they trust in space and they know that in a way, we will never be separated again. They have trust that there is life somewhere, that only a small part of space has conquered the minds, and they cannot help it but to have joy in knowing that there is life out there, and they feel this future their entire lives.

Humanoids produce telepathy.

Men do not come and want to take you with us, we do not want test samples and we do not want to do experiments. Provided that you have been abducted and tests were done to you, you have not been involved with Men, but with Others. They want to learn from humans, and they want to help humans. Many will learn through pain that there is life that they do not know. The Others usually choose as their victims those who have been refined for many generations. They take genes, and in this way many humans will meet Others every day. They can also take young men into their ships and begin interesting telepathy missions with which they search spouses for them who have been involved in experiments as well. This way they are able to continue their work in peace. In case some have been able to recover their memory, they just want to think it is all over. If they think it is over, they are mistaken. This work will continue until the end of their lives.

When you are in a situation like this, you can no longer stop. Usually, you have given permission during your sleep. When you cannot bare this, you realize that your spiritual development is not the way it should be. You should spiritually grow from these contacts. Although you are test subjects, you yourselves have wanted to be that.

You are meeting again and again with spirits that you have mistaken with humanoids.

There is a spirit world.

There are humanoids.

There are evil humanoids.

And there are Men who are also humanoids.

And there are evil humanoids that are like Men but evil.

You meet spirits who come and go as they want, and often you think that they are humanoids, but instead, they are spirits. Humanoids are not spirits, they are just as much alive as you are. Humanoids die like you do, although they are a different matter than you are. Many have thought that regular spirit beings are Men or the Others. Many live in all types of fears after they have met evil humanoids. Men will not cause even the slightest fear.

If you meet Men, you do not feel any fear, but you think that you have met with an angel or some other being from the lower levels of God's Kingdom. When you encounter other spirit beings that are also humanoids but are not evil, do what you must.

Humanoids usually come when they have some work to do with you. Try to be part of this work and overcome the thought that violence and evil is being done to you. When evil humanoids come, you are in trouble and will need help. Nobody can really survive from them without help. When you come into telepathy where you want to kill yourselves or run for your lives, you have probably become a test subject for evil humanoids. This evil humanoid is probably in contact with an evil person who is near you. They work together like the good ones work together. When you do not know what to do, you just need to learn how to pray so that your aura will be in the light, and that the imprint it leaves in the aura will prevent them from coming back. When you cannot even pray anymore, and the evil humanoids have broken your aura, you will need help from spirit beings or angels or someone who can help you. Men cannot help you if the evil humanoids have taken control over you. We cannot help because we are not in contact with evil energies anymore.

Angels have the courage to come and repair your aura, but not if the evil humanoids are nearby. Spirit beings will come when the negative energy is not present. That is why you need to go to church, or to another holy place where you can help yourselves connect with God's good energy.

Evil humanoids produce evil telepathy, sexual states, and difficult long-term fears of the dark. Red evil humanoids produce anguish and pain. Black evil humanoids produce conditions resembling mental illness and uncontrollable fits of rage. Small ones, that you can barely distinguish from one another, are mean, and they destroy tissue and cut off pieces for no reason. They do senseless experiments. They just want to destroy because what they do cannot be differentiated from the work that the Others do. When they begin to do experiments to you, or when they abduct you, then you are in much bigger trouble than you think. They want you to think that they are Others, and they will disguise themselves in a type of costume so that they look the same. They dress in fireproof red outfits, and they get fire's telepathy that has evil. When they produce their own telepathy, it is nothing but mocking and ridiculing. Every so often, someone will become their victim. Usually, there is someone evil already in their destiny and therefore they are already in big trouble.

The Others do not want to cause any suffering. The Storks do not want anyone to think that Men are these small, large eyed beings. Men are not them. Many think that the evil ones are good. Men do not do experiments or abduct people. When you get abducted by the evil ones, get in touch with a hypnotist and unlock your memory. When you do not know if the ones who abducted you were good or evil, you will notice that you and the other abductees have different types of transmissions. You are usually installed telepathic transmissions that you should be able to interpret. These transmissions reveal whether you had contact with an evil or good humanoid. If you still wish to know more about the small humanoids, we will explain more about their work.

This message was given by a humanoid.

Nothing happens without God's knowledge. Not even a hair splits from a human's head without God's knowledge. When you do not know what is happening in your life, think of what has already happened. When you think of what has already happened, you will realize that everything that has happened was something that you could not even imagine. Which one is better? To be alive, or to be dead? When you die, you do not want to die. When you are alive, you do not want to be alive, and when you come back to where you started from, you will realize that what you were in the beginning, you will no longer be in the end. Whatever you want, it will leave from you and you will realize that the time you had was not used in vain. When you do not know why you live, and what you are looking for, you could never imagine that what you are looking for is you, yourselves. You search without wanting to realize that what you are searching for is your own self that is hidden within you.

Humanoids will come back to the Earth when the time is full, and when this time has come full, you will be ready. Everyone who must be ready will be ready. Those who are not ready will not come with Men to sing, dance, and have fun with us. They will be left behind and someone else will come and pick them up, but nobody comes unless the time is full. You can think that you are ready and that everything is ready, however, nobody comes. When the time is full, there is not one body who can explain when this time is. Only God alone in Heaven knows what that time is which has to be fulfilled. Whatever happens to you, remain calm, because what happens has to happen. You do not know why, but God knows, and when your time comes in full, then you will know also.

Although it has been revealed to you about what happens in the future, you do not know when it will happen. Provided that someone who is in the light can see the future, they will not know when, and that is how it is meant for you. Nobody knows the time, or when everything is meant to happen. When it is time for things to happen, they will happen.

When you want someone to tell you why you always get disappointments and someone else gets more happiness, then you will have to begin to search for answers for which it is hard to find a true answer. First, you should look for answers from your current life, problems that bother you night and day that deprive you of happiness and prevent you from receiving love and joy. When the answers cannot be found from this life, then maybe you need to begin searching for answers from your previous lives. Maybe the answers to your unhappiness can be found there, and if you still have not found the answers, maybe you need to search for God, Who will help to find the truth.

God is in everything that you do or will do. Provided that you cannot even find God, perhaps you will find Satan who has taken a place in your life. Although you might not want to admit it, you should always be in contact with the Storks, like the Sons of God are in contact with you. Men are here to help and teach you, and when you come into our flying saucers, you will realize that everything that was said to you was true.

Humanoids have sent to exile some of us who did not have the right kind of spiritual development. They wander among you, and they do not know who they are. They once were Men, and now they live amongst you, and you do not recognize the skin and bone to be the same as yours. This means that the ones that were once us, will always remain different, like they were when they lived among us. They usually carry a mark in some body part and physically they are slender, they have many thoughts that will be foreign to you. They are not quite like we are. They are like Children of the Earth, but unfortunately, they can never live in a way like the Children of Earth. Usually, they are rather popular due to their evident abilities. Usually, they know how to produce telepathy and interpret dreams, and they go to places where they can find people who need telepathy, and they are able to send.

If they are evil, they are worse than usual. They know how to take advantage of people because they know telepathy. They make people their slaves. They shamelessly take advantage of them. Due to their apparent abilities, they can take whatever they want from people. Usually, people will make promises to them which they do not want to keep. This happens because they can bend human minds with their good skills in telepathy. When they want someone to be their slave, they normally take the kind of people who do not fight back but will blindly do as they are told. When evil humanoids have come into your lives, they will not leave you unless they want to leave you. Many love them blindly knowing that they are super humans.

There are not many who are in exile, there are only a hundred of them incarnated on Earth, and they live in different parts of the Earth so that they cannot meet each other. Many of them will become famous, and many of them are here helping human beings. Because, in a way, they are in exile, you have to pray for them so that they can return back to us. Men have found each and every one of them who are living on Earth at the moment, and they are all waiting for the completion of this book. They think very differently than humans, they can never adjust to the human thought pattern, which will always remain very strange to them.

Humanoids do not think like the Children of Earth do, like we have previously explained. We do not care about who is in power and we do not care about money. We do not love others because they are fun or beautiful, we do not care to arrange funerals that have many trusting family members. We do not care how we die, and after death the ones we leave behind are no longer important, like they are to humans.

When you do not know if you are one of us, then you are not one of us. Each one of our own has the knowledge of this, even the ones that are evil. Also, Lea has always known this, and as she got older it became even more clear to her, like she knows each one of our own know even the evil ones as she knows everyone who is one of Men, even the ones that are evil. They usually live alone, usually our own will always be lonely in their own way, even if they have a family. They can never take away the loneliness that radiates from them when they live among the Children of the Earth. When you meet them, you will know that they are one of us, you do not know who they are, but you know they are not like you.

There are many different types of humanoids and there are many different kinds of humans, and there are many reasons that can make a human different, but the way our own are different, whether man or woman, is something else entirely. They seem friendly but are difficult to approach. They are popular but they do not care about their popularity. They usually have nice appearances, but they barely think about that. Usually, they are highly intelligent, but they can create suffering with their new way of thinking. They seem spiritual even if they do not talk about spiritual things. They will usually get pupils around them whether they want that or not. They are always searching for something in their lives, they study their lives and search for something that is absent from their knowledge. While searching for a secret from their lives, they often realize that they have lived a different kind of life than humans. Their most difficult task on Earth is to be a human, and after they learn this, they will be ready to come back to us.

When you Children of the Earth think about who you are, you will realize that your place is always with God. In the dual battle of the low self and the higher self, you will finally come to rest in God's Great Kingdom that is great, and where everyone has their own land, and their own place. When your spiritual development becomes full, you can go back to all the others who left before you. Your loved ones from Earth are here and you will be happy because your development has come full.

Many of you come back here to help your own to continue their spiritual development and those who do not want to come back will go to a small star where spiritually developed Children of the Earth live. They live in a star where there is joy and an almost heavenly mood. They help by notifying their own that they are living and happy, and that they will come back whenever they are needed on Earth. They can stay in the star or they can come to let you know that they are alive. Even nowadays, they can be born back to Earth to help people learn spiritual development. When the time has come full and we come to get all Children of Earth, you who worked here to help those who were in need of help can rest in peace. All of those who did not want to help the ones who were in in trouble, or who were unhappy, will have to go to Hell, where what was brought by the evil will be burned away. When you do not realize that you are here not only for the sake of yourselves, but also for the sake of others, you have not developed as you should. When the spiritual development does not go as it should, you have to learn everything from the beginning.

Humanoids are the light. The light is the humanoids. The humanoids will bring you the light, light that is the light of the words. Through words we will bring light to the ignorance that is the darkest. We come as we have come since the beginning of humankind. After you leave, (Earth/life) you will realize that you were never alone, and that the universe is a great big ocean where each fish has its own colors.

A-A-A

Humanoids will begin.

Humanoids will come to Earth and take with them those humans whose development has reached so high that they no longer need to live here. When the time has come full, Men will come and take away all of those who are ready. We will announce it. When we come and begin this, everything will have already begun. The evil has become loose, and everything that is left is evil. There will be only a few left who are spiritually developed, and we will come and take them away. When we pick them up and take them to our flying craft, we will take them to the small star where there are spiritually developed Children of the Earth. They have always been in this planet during their sleep and they will know that all that happens, happens only because of the Earth's time that has come full. Humanoids will begin this cleansing when the has come full. Men will come to get their own and will come and get the spiritually developed Children of the Earth. The ones who are left here on Earth, a funeral is waiting for them. They can only hope that what will happen, will happen quickly.

The path that you choose is the one who makes you for who you in the end will become. When you choose wrong, you cannot always go back and start from the beginning. When finally realizing the mistakes that you have made at this point, in the pain that you will live in, you can no longer wish to go back to the beginning which no longer exists. The reincarnations, which there have been many, and that cannot be removed, are paths that you have lived like crazy. You are still given yet another chance, at the times of the end you will not be given one. What the lower self has come to announce to you is that although you will begin again, you are no longer a beginning, but only an end. When you realize that all flying craft that you will see or meet with, are all evil instead of good. You can be sure that there is not much time left. This is one sign sent by God.

In the edge of the heavens there are many Men. Some are evil. When only the evil make contact, nothing can help you anymore. The low self, the fame, and the glory that you want, but cannot take with you can help you only on a physical level and will not help you on a spiritual level. When your choices are dominated only by the body and the low self, the only thing you have is your living life. When you choose in spirit and in according to your higher self, you will be in spirit which will remain after your death. When the higher spirit cannot control what you do any more, you can no longer keep it and it will leave.

The high spirit is the spirit that God gave to each one who is born to Earth, like it was announced. Satan gave the low spirit that is Satan's like the high spirit is God's. When the high spirit has been removed, the human is being led only by the low spirit and as the low spirit evolves, the human becomes Satan's own. When we announce that the time has come full, we will explain it through telepathy. Many have taken this telepathy and created all kinds of strange history. Behind that was humanoids who wanted to warn you so that you would not think that no one is able to control you.

We have left many messages throughout your history. One, that you did not want to believe was a man who seemed intelligent, and was intelligent in every way, who explained that he had been in a flying saucer where he was being taught. He wrote a book about this. Nevertheless, nobody wanted to believe what he tried to explain. Like we can take people into our crafts and teach them, we can also teach you by explaining that we have been in contact with you through telepathy. Many have met with Men, but they do not want to talk about this, provided that we want them to speak, they will but we do not until it is their time to speak.

Humanoids will come like a thief in the night, and when you do not know, we have come. Men do not want you to know when the time has come full. Humanoids will come when the time is full, and you must be ready when we come. Provided that we come, and you are not ready, we will not come back. We will bring you a message, and through that message, you can choose what you will do, and so it has been commanded that each lower and higher being has the free will to choose what they want to choose. When you choose Satan, do not wonder if you can no longer come back to God. Humanoids come from God, so that when you are in Hell, you can trust who is there. When you choose God, you will have to go through many temptations, and you will have many situations where you must defeat Satan. You cannot come to God unless you have defeated Satan. That is why you have to defeat Satan over and over again.

A-A-A

Men are here.

We do not think like you humans do. We do not think about why everything is the way it is, we just do everything that we can. We are not saying that we would begin life without any interest, like you are interested in everything. We begin our life like you do as children and as we grow, we learn that things have to be changed both spiritually and physically. We do not begin life like we would start everything from the beginning. We start by continuing from where we left off.

When children are at school age, they leave home and will be away all the time after that so that they will learn to be separate from their parents and learn how to be independent. Parents take care of the children when they are babies and when they come to the age where they know how to speak, walk and read they will go to school where they will be given physical and spiritual teachings. When they come back home, they have detached from their parents and they know how to register them in according to what they mean to them. Provided that they are close spiritually, they will know that. They are together all those years when they are in school and they come home for holidays and vacations. Humanoids do not want to explain everything in detail.

We do not have funerals at all because the ones who die cannot prevent their departure. They should not have to feel sadness because of that. Provided that the family members are crying by their casket, it is more difficult for them to leave. After that person has left, the children can gather at their home and have a celebration in their honor. This celebration is such that where everyone who knew them can explain what they meant to them. They usually explain this to the relative who is still alive, and they will thank them for being his family. They will give support and help them. When the person who had passed away was not present but had left early, this means that he had been revealing secrets from death. Usually, the ones who left prematurely return to the living and explain about the kingdom of the dead. They can also be enlightened after death. Although usually, the enlightenment happens before death. Humanoids can also have fun. We have many occasions where we get together and have fun. Nowadays, we can cook regular food, eat and visit elderly and with them we can enlighten our own spiritual development. They know everything about anything that we do not know yet.

On a physical level, we can also influence the telepathy that comes from the spirits. (Humans who have recently passed away) They want knowledge that they do not have yet, and they can only seek a path to a new spiritual development. When they receive Men's telepathy, they want to know what they can do. Humanoids live like they have lived before the birth of the world. We were in the beginning; we will be in the end. Provided that you cannot understand this, there is nothing we can do. We cannot do more than what we have already done.

Humanoids have done a lot work for the sake of enlightenment on Earth. Provided that you do not want to know about the things we have done, we cannot help you to expand your consciousness. We do not know how to think like you do. We do not try, and we do not want to live like you. We are not selfish, and we do not want to own anyone, or hurt anyone with our bodies. When we come to life, we get what we deserve. When one is funny, one is funnier, and the third is beautiful, and we Men are intelligent. We just think that we get what is meant for us. We do not think that God is mistaken when He does not give everyone the same. We never doubt God. If someone would, they would not be one of us.

When we begin our spiritual development, we always begin it from ourselves, not from another person like you do, but from ourselves. We live by examining ourselves, and by searching for ourselves we will find. When we realize who we used to be, and what the lower level we were, then the more we want to develop. When we begin our spiritual development, we always come to a time when we were not as developed as we are now. This is how we know whether or not we have learned anything. We do not necessarily have karma, if we do, it is very slight. Someone can have bad energy just because they were not students of the Sons of God. Men teach about the evil energy because we have been in contact with the Children of the Earth. Evil energy does not come amongst us, but if someone does not want to know about it, they can get it. To be able to learn everything that is, is for the sake of learning. Nobody forces anyone to learn, and nobody is forced into spiritual development. Everyone themselves wants to do these things as we have previously explained. When we cherish the love that we have, we would never say that the love that we have is better or worse.

When we cherish love, it is like a veiled woman near whom there is happiness and whom you can never see clearly. Love is a secret which bonds we do not want to open. When we love, we cherish this love until it becomes the only thing we do not want to leave. When Men leave with our flying craft, we do not take our wives with us. They will wait until we return. They would rather choose this long wait than to be together with someone else. (Note from the translator, this text apparently was written years before, because an earlier text in this book it says that the wives can come to the craft to do the same work, these journals were not dated.)

We have also made mistakes that we will later explain. We have to pay a high price for our mistakes. That is why we do not want to make mistakes. We want to know what we want and only do what is right. Provided that we do not think the way we need to think, nowadays, we have to leave. First, we will learn things in the flying craft that are near the Earth, and after that, we will begin the reincarnations of the Path of the Four Fires, where a few of us there have lived.

If we still have not learned in the harmony of the low self and of the high self, then in our latitude there are many different planets where we can place this rebel, unless they have fallen to Satan. When everything is good again, they can come back to their own. When we lose one of our own to Satan, this is a great loss. We do not want to lose even one, which will cause murderous horrible vibrations. Creation of the new will never replace the loss of the old.

God is creative, and He creates in such a way that He does not rest. When He does rest, Satan can do his work. This is called co-operation, which you cannot understand. When God rests, Satan works, when Satan is resting, God is working. Only those who do not know God or Satan can imagine that God never rests.

In a way, He does not rest, but He will allow things to happen, and that is His rest. A providence that prevents and allows things to happen. His work is not to keep control over a human's spiritual development, that work belongs to the humans. When the human does not want to develop, he will go and follow Satan. When you do not know what God is, and what Satan is, then you are not part of the spiritual development, and you are not following God. Everyone who lives on Earth has to be conscious of Satan. When Satan takes his own, he no longer asks, "Are you going to follow me?", he just comes and takes away his own. Unless you want to be his disciple, do not hesitate to look for God, and do not doubt that Satan exists and will take his own.

There is a lot of evil on Earth. What is threatening is the one who is too afraid to realize that. When you choose, you always choose from two. You always have two choices. When you make a choice that is not physical or spiritual, then it is satanic. Whether you want it or not, you make choices throughout your entire life. When you do not care about what you choose, then you do not know who you are. No one of God's own is like that. You know what it means when God's own are faced with a choice. They know what to do, they will always ask, "Is this the right choice?", and they do not explain afterwards that they did not know what they did.

There are many different planets. Each one has their own connections. Different planets have their own spiritual teachings and their own communities. Many live very differently than us. That is why you cannot think that everyone who you meet are Men. We live under our own laws, and they live under their laws of the body and spirit. Provided that you meet other ones, and they want to teach you, learn what you can from them. They also want to help humans like others whom you cannot see. Provided that they do not harm you, you can also learn from them.

Many are not quite like Men, and many are not quite like humans. When they teach you, then learn, but do not think that they are the only ones who exist. When their work has been accomplished, they will leave, and other ones will come after. They have come and the ones who are physically different will come, and after, the kinds of whom you have not met. They will all come to teach from their flying saucers. Humanoids have been fun and physically different. When our time comes, we will come and when we begin our contacts you will know that we are here. After us, only the evil ones will come, and when the evil ones come, you will know that the time is full.

Humanoids produce telepathy, this one was Cirius.

A-A-A

Children of Earth, creation is only a temporary place where you can grow. There have been many flying saucers, and there have been many Men here. Humanoids are here to help you.

You do not know what love and hate is. You do not know who is a loved one, and who is an enemy. You do not know your own whom you meet, and you do not know anything about your bodies. You have a body that lives its own life independently. Unless with a lot of work and effort, you overcome your body, it will overcome you. You cannot be the slaves of your own bodies. When you do not overcome your body, it will overcome you. Once it has control over you, you are no longer who you are supposed to be. The way you are supposed to be is that you can control your own lives, take care of yourselves, that you can love as a spirit, and that you know how to be like one who wanted to be spiritually developed. When you claim that you are spiritually developed, you are not spiritual developed. Nobody who is spiritually developed wants to make a big deal about it.

Humanoids met a man who insisted that he was spiritually developed. This man lived in his own house and lived like a hermit. He wanted to teach spiritual development so he put an ad in a newspaper so that he could teach spiritual development. When people came to him, he explained to them that they must stop smoking cigarettes, that they must stop having sex, and that they have to stop living near other people. They did as they were told and after no more students came to him, the man left to look for his students. When he found them they were very unhappy. They considered themselves to be good, but they were not happy. When they asked if this is the purpose of life, the man replied, "Just as the light is there next to you, it is also within you, and when you place the light and come into a space within, then you have awakened in spirit.". This was the truth we had taught him. When you place the light within yourself, and as you become conscious of the light, you will be a part of spiritual development.

When this happened, the students wanted to know what they should do next. The man put one student outside of his house, and another inside the house and asked, "Which one is the body, and which is this who speaks?" When the man who was outside said, "The one who speaks is the body, and the one who is not inside the house is the spirit.", the man replied, "Not true, the man inside the house is the spirit, and the man who went outside of the house was the other man's spirit, and the one who speaks is the owner of the house, who is me, and I am the body." This story's teaching is that unless you know the low spirit, then you do not know who the one teaching you is. The low spirit is also a host that can take control over you. When you think that spiritual development is to stop smoking cigarettes, or that you live separated from other people, or that you stop having sex, you are wrong. None of that has anything to do with spiritual development. When you live just a regular life, you learn what life teaches you. When you no longer want to learn, then you have spiritually stopped developing. Development is learning from each day and from each living being.

Humanoids have thought that you cannot be happy unless you are with someone all the time. Human beings have always been together with someone from the beginning. When you have to be alone, you become unhappy, and when you can not find the right company, you will take anyone to fill your loneliness because you think that loneliness is worse than whoever you are with. When you are too afraid to be alone, you do not know yourselves. You do not know who you are, and it frightens you. You run away from yourselves in every way, and when you are too afraid to awaken the truth, you will wake up again in the same dream you were in in your past life. Everything will continue until you have the courage to wake up and look at who you are and what you want from life. When you learn this, you will slowly begin to develop spiritually. You cannot awaken your spirit or develop it with external things.

Spiritual development is the most secret thing there is in life. Nobody knows about someone else's spiritual development. When you meet a spiritually developed person, supposing that you ever will, you will realize that there is something in them that you have not realized before. Spiritually developed people do not want to bring their development in the light. They want to keep their development to themselves. Usually, they are regular people who do not want to create any impressions of themselves.

Spiritually developed people usually live for things that are close to earth, like love and art. Through art they want to give a part of themselves, and through love, they want to teach about love. When they come back to continue the work that they are doing in their new reincarnation on the Path of the Four Fires, they continue from where they left off. They never start the same life from the beginning. Normally, their reincarnations are difficult, and they develop spiritually. They are strong, although they are modest. When you do not know who you are, and what your spiritual development is, you have to begin to study yourselves. Really search for who you are and what you really want, and through the help of your body, you can find out who controls who. If your body is in control, then you are not really in charge of the things that you should be able to control. When the body takes over control you can no longer prevent it.

It wants to eat.

It wants to drink.

It wants to make love to other bodies.

It wants to take control over everything that you do.

When you do not care about who the leader is, the body can overpower you.

When your body wants you to no longer know who is absent, you no longer want to know.

Humanoids produce telepathy, and this was Adam.

A-A-A

The body is only time which we receive when we are born on Earth. When the time has come full, we will leave it and continue forward. When you do not realize that you have to learn the things that you came here to learn, and instead you live the wrong way, you will come to Earth over and over again, and your lives become even worse. When you realize that you are here to learn, you will spiritually grow, and you will have a better life. When you realize why you have the problems that you have, then you have realized a lot. This is usually the most difficult thing to learn. To become content with what you have instead of wanting something that is not meant for you. When you realize that what you get is according to who you are, then you have learned a lot. When you want what is not meant for you, you will meet your lower selves. This low self will gradually take over you. That is why you should learn how to hold important what you already have and learn what you are supposed to learn from it.

When the lower self takes over you, you cannot control your life anymore, but it will control you. When the low self begins to control you, you will soon realize that you no longer know what you are doing. When you no longer know what you are doing, you will be even more controlled by the low self. Through this, the evil spirits, and other spirits come that want to influence your life. So, do not think that what you did not have from the beginning was not what was meant for you. When you no longer want anything that is not meant for you, you realize that you are happy and free. You can live as you should. When you live through what you have to, then you will learn what you have to learn and when you have learned what you have to, there will be physical and spiritual change. This is why you should not want things that are not meant for you.

When you meet someone who is asking for promises from the past and future from you, do not stay thinking with your body. You cannot know a person unless you get to know them, and when you know them, then you know who they are. Nobody can ask for promises of the future and the past. There is no such law in the world. Once you get to know the person who you think you love, you might not love them. That is why you do not vow for love that you do not know. When you know who you love, then you can say that you love them.

What is truth, is the truth. The truth will never change, it will always remain. Nothing through the laws of the body or spirit can change it. When you live on Earth and meet a lot of people who do not have any friends, befriend them because you never know when your life will reach that same point. When you do not know what the future holds for you, then how can someone else know it? When you want to know about the future, do not believe in everything that you are being told. When you believe it, you might fulfill what was told to you. When you do not believe, then you can freely do what you have to.

When you come into your body, you are given many opportunities. Everyone will have many choices to choose from, but unfortunately, when you do not want to make the right choices, many opportunities will be lost. Humanoids helped a man who wanted to die. We came to speak to the man and explained that this was because of his own choices. If he would make the right choice, he would live a better life. When the man realized that he had been guided by his lower self, he did not want to die anymore. He wanted to start everything from the beginning and learn to know himself. When you have learned to know yourselves, you know who you are and what you are learning. Maybe you are not the one who has to become famous and learn from that, but maybe you are the one who has become spiritually rich and will learn from that. Whatever is in your destiny, learn from it. What you will learn in this life you do not have to learn in the next.

This was written by Cirius.

Bye, Bye.

A-A-A

Children of the Earth, come and do what you have to do. You do not just live here, you also live in the second plane which you are not familiar with. Men know you better than you know yourselves. Men know what you are thinking and what you want, but when we cannot prevent you, there is nothing that with our bodies we can do to help you. You can freely do what you want to do, but you will soon realize that everything has its price. When you make the wrong choice, you have to pay the price for that wrong choice. When you do not think about what you do, then you do not know what happens and why. When you do not care about who you are, and you think, "Everything is next to nothing" you create a lot suffering around you. When you think this thought, "That although you do not care about what happens, you can be in peace regardless of what you do." Then you have joined Satan. No one can prevent him from getting you when the time is full.

Provided that you do not know how to live right, and that everything you do went wrong, then you probably do not know yourselves, and you did not know what was right for you. It is important that you know yourselves so that you do not make the wrong choices for that reason.

Provided that you want to know yourselves, you will come to a time where you know your past living life. You will have to know this life that you lived earlier.

A-A-A

Men produce telepathy.

We do not love you humans like Jesus did. We are not like He was. We think and live differently than you do. We want you to know that you are a part of Satan, and a part of God. We are not here to sacrifice ourselves to your Satan. Crazy is the one who thinks to be part of God through their low selves when they are a part of Satan.

Men produce this telepathy.

When you find out who you are, then you can make your choice consciously. After that, you no longer have the mercy you had before you knew who you were. When you become conscious of yourselves, then you can only make a choice of whose side you are on. After that, you are what you are. When your time has come full, you will go with who you served. Then, you no longer have to think about how crazy the one is who imagines to be under the control of an evil spirit. Crazy is the one who is too scared to believe that the bad spirits exist and will come and get their own.

Humanoids have come here only so that you will learn that you are not super humans, and that you are nothing more than Satan's created low spirits. Also, God in His mercy gave you a spirit, but that spirit will die unless you keep it alive through prayers. Your actions, choices and proper thinking will keep the spirit God gave you alive. When you partake in heinous joys and only want evil, the spirit will die, and you will just be a part of Satan. When you become free from evil and in fire you will burn clean, then you will come back to God. This means that you have defeated the evil in your own selves. As we have previously explained, you will come to a time where you will have made a choice, either the right one, or the wrong one. According to that, you will be judged.

When you do not care about what you do, you are no longer of God. When you do not care about what happens, then you are no longer in the balance of the body and the spirit. When the spirit cannot guide you anymore, you will be left in the mercy of the body, and when through pain, the body takes over you, it will gradually through the body give the power to the lower self. Once the lower self has conquered you, then comes the evil spirits and then Satan himself.

When you have a lot of difficulties in your life, you have to think about how these difficulties came into your life. Usually, they came into your life because of your own choices. When you do not want to think about what is leading your life, then you do not care who is leading your life.

When you come into the time where you were children, you will go back to the beginning in which you started from. If you had many problems in your childhood, you have to find the reasons why you had them. Maybe you wanted to come to Earth to gain knowledge about what happened to you as a child so that you could spiritually develop better. When you do not want to learn, then you have not learned. When you do not want to learn, nobody can force you. You are here to learn things that you did not learn from the previous levels of life. When the time comes full, you will be weighed on a scale, and when the development that is in you swings towards evil you will go to Satan who will take you. Provided that your spiritual development has been right, you will become a part of God's Great Kingdom where each one always has their own part. Humanoids believe that everyone who believes in Jesus will be saved, but the faith of the body is not the faith of the spirit. Jesus spoke about the spirit, that although the spirit is strong, the body is weak. When you have defeated the body, there will still be difficult times in the spirit plane, and when you get old and you do not care about bodily pleasures, your body is not yet conquered. The body must be overcome when it is still young and full of desires.

The old man that we spoke about in the beginning had been handsome and strong when he was young, but he did not allow his body to lead his life and because of that, he was still spiritually developed, although he did not want to believe in life after death.

You learn what you have to. You are monkeys that do not have anything else but brains and not even your body is all that attractive. You will wake up to realize that you are nothing but animals, although animals are more pure than you are. With the absence of the low self, a monkey is a purer animal than what you are.

What can we teach you when you are not willing to learn? Other things that we can teach you are not willing to learn. When we teach you, we do not teach you out of the love that Jesus had for you, we teach you because it is the will of God. When God says that we have to go and speak to you, we will do it. When we do not feel love for you, we can't help finding you repulsive. We are different and we do not have such thoughts as you do. God loves all lower-level beings as you know. He let Jesus come and speak to you and you killed Jesus. For that reason, we do not have to love you. Jesus was a man who is one of us.

Humanoids can see the suffering you cause to our own and to others who have come to help you. What are you doing to everyone who needs help? What are you doing to animals? What will you do in the future? What makes you do all of that evil? It is the Satan in you, and when there is Satan in you, we do not have to love you. We do not have to love Satan. When you realize that Satan is leading your lives, you will realize that the Storks are the ones you do not want to meet. That is why you should not play stupid, and do not pretend to be good, but be who you are. When you do not play dumb, and you do not pretend to be good, you will no longer do evil to those who you have come to destroy.

When one day you no longer know what good is, and what evil is, you are in big trouble. Because of this, be evil when you are evil, and be stupid if you cannot understand, but do not pretend that you are good if you are not. Nothing is worse than good that is evil. That is directly from Satan. When you want God to guide your lives, learn one very important thing, you are both of evil and of good. When you do not want to believe that there is evil in you, you will be in its power. When you study the evil in you then you might even defeat it, otherwise you will be defeated by evil.

One of Satan's missions is to cause pain. When you cause pain to others you are Satan's helper. When you no longer want to cause pain, you will stop causing it. When you want to help and learn how to love, you will help, and you will learn how to love. When the desire to help and love is almost dead in humans, there is not much of God left. When you want to help, you help, and it does not cause pain but instead, those whom you help will get better.

The old man was tired of battling his own mind and finally went to church. When the priest was speaking, the old man thought, "What does he think he knows?" When the priest stopped speaking, the old man went to the priest and said, "When you haven't even been with a woman, how do you know what temptation is?" The priest replied, "Go away Satan." Neither the priest or the man was evil, but the man was better because he had lived through temptation and overcame it. That is why there is nobody who can be better or worse except the one who has defeated Satan. You will finally realize that you cannot become clean other than living the life that you have been given. If you do not survive this, you will finally realize that you have had many opportunities to do better and repent.

This was written by Adam.

Bye, Bye.

A-A-A

Here on Earth, there are a lot of problems. There are some who want to harm, and others who want to cause pain and suffering, and then there are the those whose only job is to serve evil. When you meet crazy people every day and wonder what has happened to them, remember that they are no longer there. Evil spirits have taken their body and driven them to madness, that is all that is left. When you do not think that the body wanders here on Earth on its own time, you do not realize that it also wants to sing and dance. The body only lives that one life that it is given. For this reason, the body also wants to be happy. If the body feels bad all the time it will put itself in a state where you cannot manage it. Under the laws of the body, it wants to enjoy all that it can.

It can eat.

It can drink.

It can sing.

It has fun the way it knows how to have fun. It wants to be loved, it wants to be admired and it wants to feel the closeness of another body. When you do not let it enjoy anything then it only wants to sleep and make your life difficult. When you do not care about your body at all, then it will begin rebellion. When you wake up, it does not want to wake up. When you stay up, it wants to sleep. When you only transmit your own thoughts, it will start bullying you. It will start whispering that you are only a body and that you are so horrible that you do not care about anything. It can also somehow with its physical ability, begin to destroy your beauty. It can cause you to age prematurely and make your appearance look messy. All of this can simply be the body's rebellion. When the body is happy you can be in joy by sleeping well and staying up. You will begin to look beautiful and will be healthy and happy. This is why you have to cooperate with your body as well. When you want to keep your body happy, you have to take care of it and give it enough rest and take it outside when you can. It is also good to teach it how to swim and enjoy the sun. You can also tell it nice stories about how another body wants to love it. That is when it becomes happy, because it also wants to be loved. When you can help the body realize that you are the boss and the body is the servant, by doing so the body will obey you and only want the best for you. When the body does not want to obey you and it thinks that you are bad, it will want you to go away. That is when it begins the rebellion. It will get sick and begin to cause you all kinds of problems. Nowadays, you will begin telepathy with a body that only wants to pray. This kind of body only wants you to no longer do the things you used to do so that it would not have to feel what it had to feel before.

(Lea, it is me Cirius. I am the same one who was here earlier today. Do you remember? I came from the door and held your hand and said it is me Cirius. I did that to Lea today when you were on the sofa and you thought that you were awake, but you were asleep. That is when I came and explained that today I started a new practice and this one who is here is Cirius. We come when you do not know and leave when you do not know. When you know when we come and go, you will remember everything. When we first met, you were very little. You always felt bad after we left. You were always so happy when we came to you, and after we left you were quiet and wanted to be alone. When we came back you got very happy and started to sing, and you wanted to come with us, but we could not take Lea with us because Lea had work to do on Earth. When you grew older you got very lonely)

When you realize that all bodies have always been together, but not the spirits, you will realize what the marriage of the body and the spirit is. When the spirit loves another spirit, the body loves this body. This is a law that you cannot prevent. When the body loves another body, it wants the body that it loves. When the spirit loves another spirit, it will only sleep and wake up to meet the one it has to. This is why you do not know about love. You think that you do.

The body does not know how to love eternally. It wants to enjoy many different bodies, but the spirit only loves once. When the spirit loves it can never stop loving. When you meet a spirit who your spirit loves, you can never stop loving. It will continue and continue for the rest of your lives and into your next lives. This kind of love you do not know about, where you want to leave it all because of this spirit. You feel such love that you want to love this spirit until the end of your life. When you do not know when such love has come into your lives, then you have not encountered it. Once you have met your spiritual love, you will know that you have met. You can pretend that you live in spiritual love, but you do not.

Like we have explained above, in your new way of thinking you think that everything you feel is love. How can you feel love when you have never loved anyone? When you feel love you no longer doubt. The body is not always in such planes as the spirit is. The body wants its own and the spirit wants its own. When you learn to separate that the love of the body is different, then you will know what the love of the spirit is and what the love of the body is. The spirit does not live its life like the body does. It does not want such things as the body does. This causes many conflicts in everyone's lives. When the body wants something that the spirit does not, you will have a lot of problems. Provided that in the future you cannot tell the difference and distinction between the body and the spirit, maybe through the low spirit you are not able to feel it anymore. The low spirit lives in the body's terms, not the high spirit. When you want to learn the difference between the will of the body and the will of the spirit, you must learn one important lesson. Do not ever think that you are only a spirit, you are a spirit and then a body, and after that comes the low self.

When the body lives in between the vibrations of these two, (high self/low self) it will always be destructive and crazy. It cannot handle the wandering of such spirits, which it is forced to experience. The low self will allow it to do whatever it wants, and the high spirit will force it to want things that will only cause the body suffering. Provided that you want your body to live in harmony, then defeat the low spirit's influence and allow the harmony to influence the joy that the body can also experience.

When the high spirit is in power, the body can feel that everything is in order. When you are sick all the time, then you should start thinking about what it is about. If you cannot find an answer, then begin a meditation with which you can learn when you were right and when you were wrong. This meditation can be hell for someone who can never get their body in control. This meditation works in the type of plane where you can silence your body completely. After this, you will know what your worst mistake was that made your body rebel. Those who also want meditation with their mind can never have peace with their own selves. They are never able to just be quiet. Such people cannot have peace from their body and are always coming and going. When you cannot just be still, something is wrong.

You need to learn how to be completely quiet and become a part of this future that lies within you. When you can be silent and you are resting and you just want to be, you are a short path away from this meditation. When you begin to feel that this is the meditation, you are wrong. This is only the beginning. When you are silent and relaxed and you can be without any thoughts, you can give this to all of your thoughts, leave all thoughts away from your mind and then you can leave your mind and sleep like children in the sea of silence. As you are sleepy, you will slowly fulfill in that energy with which you came here with. This energy is the light energy that you already have. You return back to this light and as you become a part of this light, you will become a part of spiritual development. When you first learn this, you cannot think, and you have to drive away all thoughts. After that, you sleep while awake, you remain silent as you would be in a dream, but you are awake. When you are in a dream-like state you will leave your body and come to the energy that you came from, your own aura. As you are in your own aura, you can still continue your journey towards the light given by God, and through this, you can grow.

Humanoids live here on Earth like you humans do. When we come to Earth we live like you do. We do things like you and make wrong choices many times when we live as humans.

When we make choices with our bodies, we will have to pay a price for these choices. When Men come onto Earth, we are not quite like those who are not one of us. When we come to Earth, things will happen that will not happen to you. We only come if we have made mistakes while living here. Then those who are living in the flying crafts will have to come and be born on Earth to reconcile our mistakes. Therefore, you should never be evil to the ones that are not like you are. Maybe you can never understand them but try to be friendly to them so you will not get bad karma for yourselves. When you hurt one of our own badly, you will have a lot of bad karma ahead of you. When you cannot understand them, just let them be as they are. When you do not know who is one of us, you will never know who you are. When you choose wrong and you have to pay a price for this choice, then do not wonder why. Nobody who has made wrong choices will know that until they have had to pay the price that follows.

You could think in a different way if you would know that you also have a spirit, and you can make choices through your spirit. For this reason, search for the spirit from yourselves and learn to know yourselves so that you know who you are and what you should do.

When you come into life and you want to learn the things that you came here to learn, do not under any law allow anyone to prevent your spiritual development. When someone wants to prevent your spiritual development, they do not operate under God's but Satan's laws. This should help you when you think of what you should do.

The purpose of everything is spiritual development. Only what teaches you spiritually, makes you more spiritual and what helps you to learn things best spiritually. When you realize that all joys you have are only the joys of the body, and that you are not spiritually awake, then through pain your body has taken power over you. This will never happen without pain. Each spirit will feel pain whether you want to or not if they cannot develop further. When you have learned what you need to and you have made the right choices, then you can enjoy a life that can give you peace and good feelings.

Provided that you seem happy, but you do not feel happy, then you are not happy. Happiness is when you do not feel bad or anxious and that you do not feel hatred or bitterness. It is when you can openly control your own life in all of its stages and all of its events by making sure nothing is wrong anymore. You can have peace when you think about your death, and you can be alone if you have to without it causing you any feelings of pain. When you are in harmony with your own lives, then you can be happy. If you have had a difficult life and you do not want to think about it, then you have not learned what you have to. Difficulties in your lives indicate that you have had a lot to learn. When you have had a lot to learn, you have to know what it was so that you will know what you are learning.

When you want to start everything from the beginning, first find out what went so badly wrong. This way you will not make the same mistakes again. If you still make the same mistakes, then you have not learned what you should, but if you want you can always start from the beginning. God forgives many times and He also gives a new beginning. When you are given a new beginning, be careful, maybe it is an ordeal or tribulation that you have to overcome. There is no purpose that everything that looks good would be good. Evil will never come and say that I am evil, you can only learn through time what evil and good is. When you are searching for an easy way out and you go to someone who knows the future, do not believe all that you are being told because what is easy is easy, and that is not what life is. When you have become free from searching for happiness from everyone else you will soon drift to a time where you will do what you are doing now, what has happened today, has also happened in your past life. So, keep that in mind so that you will not do the same things too many times, so that this life that you are living now will not be your last.

Humanoids produce telepathy and this one was sent by Cirius.

Bye, Bye.

A-A-A

Men come here, we are producing telepathy from a flying craft and this is produced by Adam. We do not live like you humans do. We work and do things through our bodies like you do. The body is just a vessel for us, not the purpose itself. Year after year, through our bodies, we do what we have to in according to the situation. For us, a new body is just a tool that we use, like you use all the tools that you have. When we no longer need it, we will go to the second plane and we live there. By this we mean death, that you are so afraid of. When we leave the body, we come back when we are allowed to come back, in reality this means that we will come back when all of our other loved ones have come back.

We can always live near those who we love and because of this we never have to live lonely. We come back at the same time with all of our loved ones. We live in perfect harmony with one another. When we meet, we do not cause pain, nor do we open anything that is not permitted. When you make spells, you will be in big trouble. This means that you will not get the body or the spirit that was meant for you, and that is why the things that you want are not the best for you. Provided that with a spell you take what you want, which usually does not work, but if it does work, your karma will be such that you cannot close your eyes without Satan being there ready to take you because you have done a lot of spells. The effect of the evil is in the telepathy. You will come to a telepathy with Satan who will take you when your time is full. Provided that you do not start doing spells in your next life, that you might still get, you cannot live in peace during day or night. You will have to escape Satan chasing you everywhere. When you finally realize what you have done, you will have to keep yourselves in the light and you cannot do anything that will take the pain away without God's mercy. Provided that you do not know what you have done in your past life, then you do not know what is happening to you. When things are happening and you cannot find the reasons why, then the reasons might lie in your past life. When you do not know what to do, then do all that you can. Learn from everything that you live through. Maybe through learning you can reconcile for what you have done.

When you are not quite sure of who you are, you will come to the time where you came on Earth. You were given a body and a new life. When you get to know your life, you will feel something deep within you.

In the heavens there are many different kinds of beings and many different forms of existence of which you have no idea. Many come from different stars so that they learn what they must. Those who have come from these stars are usually very intelligent, and they normally have some gifts that cannot be achieved through the body. They know how to produce telepathy and they are very talented. Usually, they know how to compose music and they know how to sing differently than humans. Some know how to paint, and some are just otherwise talented. Usually, these types of people are envied because people realize that they are not human. Their talents are different from others in such ways that they are not like humans. When they search for a spouse, they usually cannot find one that is right for them. They usually cannot be very happy in a way a human may be. They search for an answer to why they are too different to be able to be happy like humans are. When they cannot find answers, they might become an alcoholic or even start using drugs to be able to find the harmony they cannot find otherwise. Usually, they are just very lonely. They can have many friends, but they never feel like they belong to any group, depending on their status, they are lonely. Many have become rich and very famous but that does not help them to become happy. They just feel like they live outside of everything else without any explanation. This can also be a point for such a life that has reached a resolution. When the human has developed far enough, it will be difficult for them to find company for themselves.

When you do not know what your problem is, then search for reasons and remain completely honest. As you begin searching for reasons, you have to study your life when your life has always been strange and events in your life have always been different than others. Then most likely you have come from space. When space humans live on Earth, they are usually not allowed to meet their own. This is because of millions of different reasons. Usually, if they get to meet their own, they cannot develop in such a way as wished. That is why you will meet the ones who you are supposed to meet.

If you have met someone who can make you happy, then for sure you are not a space human. In this way, you also can learn who you are.

Space humans can of course live like the Children of Earth as well, but they cannot feel such joy and happiness as the humans who find each other. When you realize that presumably you are a space human, then you need to understand that you are learning about human life, that you also learn from Satan and that you learn to love other lower beings. When you are freed from your body then you can return to your own. When your life is difficult it is a question of your promise to love and defeat Satan. That is what you knew when you came here on Earth.

The body is an enormous machine that has many different parts.

It is both holy and unclean.

It is both good and evil.

It is often in trouble, and it constantly wants something.

When you do not know the body, it will overpower you and it will want you to allow it to do whatever it wants. When it is holy, you have cleansed it from its desires, and you have liberated it from the power of the mind. When you do not know your body, you are in trouble. Nobody can conquer the body without knowing it. How can you know what the problem with the body is or what the problem of the spirit is unless you know your own body?

Humanoids will begin telepathy after you rest and would like to continue again.

This was written by Adam and Cirius.

Bye, Bye.

A-A-A

Me are here.

Only Men can send telepathy. Others cannot do that because they are not in such a vibrational level. Although we can produce telepathy, we cannot provide answers to questions that are too difficult. We can send telepathy that comes directly from the brain that we have placed previously. This telepathy does not come directly. We have placed it earlier in Lea's brain. Humanoids are not automatic writings that come from the spirit world. Automatic writings do exist, and Lea can also do such writings, but as she allows some spirits to enter her aura, there is always the danger that an evil spirit can come through. The spirit world is never completely trustworthy. Humanoids do not use the aura body but instead we will place this text in her brain. When Lea is asleep, we come and place this in her brain. When we come and begin a contact that is verbal, (Note from the translator, these verbal contacts continued for several years and some of the contents of those messages, are at the end of this book.) what we do to be able to establish these verbal contacts is that we will leave our bodies and step inside Lea's body. When these connections are born, she is always very happy because she wants this connection to happen and when we do this she feels joy and happiness. When we go inside the body, we normally travel from afar and it takes a lot of work to be able to achieve it. When we do that, she will become very happy very fast, we only come when we have to, and when we have something important to say.

Humanoids produce telepathy.

When you like someone who is not one you can love, then do not think that it is serious love. When you do not know what love is, and what it is not, then do not do anything. If you cannot trust yourself, then you cannot trust someone else's feelings either.

Humanoids create telepathy.

When you have lifelong relationships, you cannot want other bodies. When you want other bodies, and you believe that your love is serious, then you do not love anyone, and you might never learn how to love. When you do not know why you cannot love anyone, maybe you have not met anyone who would be right for you. When you do get the opportunity, do not leave it behind, take what is meant for you.

A-A-A

We are coming here, and we create telepathy. When you choose, you will always come to the telepathy that Men create.

Men create this telepathy.

We do not cause any pain, nor do we cause any evil. When we come here, we only come to help from our flying crafts, and we want you to finally realize that not everyone from space is here to do honest work or to help. There are also many evil humanoids whose only purpose is to cause problems and more suffering, of which you already have enough of here on Earth. We cannot help you unless you help yourselves first. Humanoids come from the light. We are the senders of the light. Humanoids are Men that are working in between the Earth and the edge of the heavens. We are here to work, and we want to help those of you that are searching for help.

You have a lot of problems here on Earth. You have a lot of suffering and many tribulations, and there is a lot of evil. Only through the light can you overcome the darkness. When evil things are done to you and they hurt you, you need to search for the light from God, with whose help you can overcome the pain. When you do not have the strength to fight anymore, you always have to overcome the mind. You must overcome the mind that you have. This mind helps you to stay attached to the pain. Provided that you do not know how to become free from the mind, you have to find someone as your guide who can help you. They usually come into your lives in one way or another when your time for mercy has come full. When you realize that you no longer want to live the way you used to, then you will usually be given mercy and you will be helped. When you receive help then accept it. When you do not want to receive the help you are given, then you can no longer complain about why God does not help you.

Humanoids are here.

We do not want you to think that it is right to play with fire. When you do not care about when you play with fire, you no longer care about anything. For this reason, whoever reads the Bible and plays with fire, with all honesty, is the one who will never arrive at the right place at the right time. What this means is that the one who serves two masters always cheats the other, and when you cheat on one, you also cheat the other. The ones like that can never be anything in the realms between the body and the spirit. When you meet the type of people who do not know on whose side they are on, be strict with them so that they learn from right and wrong. When you do not care about what you do to them, then you will get bad karma from their spiritual development.

If you do not know what you should do, go to a place where you can find many spiritually developed people and learn what they can teach you. When you do not know what you should do, learn how to meditate and search for help from God, and if you still do not know, then search until you find. When you just do not know what is right and what is wrong, always be awake and see what happens. When evil happens, you are wrong and when good happens, you are right. When you cannot know why everything happens, then you have to find the explanation from your past. In your past, you will come back to the time where you made wrong choices. When you learn that you cannot live through your low selves, then you are searching for your higher selves. When through your high self you learn that you will come to a time when you were not a body, but nothing else than a spirit, you will realize that the body lives its own life, and the spirit its own, and that you have to learn to distinguish the difference between the body and the spirit. When the body becomes strong, it only wants to be in a joyful life, it wants to eat and drink, and it cries about how it wants and wants. When you do not want to teach it to be your servant, it will do what it wants, and you will come to a pain that you cannot remove. This pain is created when the spirit does not have the strength to fight against the power of the body. It will become more fragile, and when it dies it will return to God's light and will stop developing. It will become a part of the energy where it once came from, and it only wants to be a part of God. The body can still continue to live after that.

According to a study we did on Earth, there are many who only have a hole and no longer a spirit. Replacing the spirit, there is only a plain hole. These types of people only live for sex and food, and they are as if they were mentally deficient. They just exist and do not know how to think or know much about anything. They can be recognized when you try to talk with them. They are not able to hold a sensible conversation. They just exist and want to eat. They usually dress strangely because the body wants to look fancy. For them, things that are fun are working, eating, drinking and some other little physical things. Sex is fun for them and they have it as often as they can. Usually, they are not evil, they are just spiritless and no longer have a spirit. The body will continue to live on its own until the end. When you meet them, you will realize that they are nobody. They just are, and as they grow old, they will normally lose all knowledge of who they are. Finally, they will just die away. Bodies like this can be ordinary people or be a little crazy. They are not evil anymore, although they once were. This evilness is what drove the spirit back to God's light, and the spirit has shattered and gone back to the beginning.

The ones that become evil are different. They have allowed their lower selves to become independent, and this low self will eventually go to hell where it came from. A person who has spiritual development will continue to grow and his body is a vessel with which he can fulfill himself. The development will continue and continue until the spirit grows even greater and materializes into the second level where it can continue the spiritual development. This second level is a space, where the consciousness is so great that it can receive even more development. When you do not know what you should do to be sure of your own development, begin a meditation where you are in the light to allow your spirit to grow and become stronger so that it will be able to control your life.

When life is difficult and you no longer know what is right and what is wrong, then trust in God who will guide you. When you do right you will feel it, and when you do wrong you will feel it. You will learn that everything that happens only happens so that you can learn. Life is for the sake of learning. You did not come here just to have fun. When you just want fun things, then you have not developed as you should have.

This was written by Cirius.

Bye, bye.

A-A-A

We come and begin this if you are ready. When you feel that the time is ready you can begin.

Men have produced telepathy, we come when the time is full. Men come and produce telepathy.

There are many humanoids here on Earth. Others are different. Men do not come through the low self, Men only come through the higher self. We can also come and speak to the crazies and dumb, but it will not help us, and it will not help them. When we want to leave a message, we come here and explain what the message is. Other people can only connect through their body to the ones who have come from outer space. There are also others who will come here from other solar systems and they also want you to take their telepathy. There are many kinds of humanoids that are unknown to you.

We cannot always help you Children of the Earth from our flying crafts. You are in big trouble with evil spirits. It is very difficult to get rid of them when you do not even acknowledge that you have many spirits in you and you cannot help yourselves or anyone else. When you want these spirits to leave, you cannot get rid of the body that you have. This body that has gotten used to these inhabitants will not allow your spirit in anymore. You think that ever since you were little you have had many different types of personalities, one is happy, the other is different and the third something else. You do not even realize that you have many different spirits in your body. For this reason, you have a lot of problems. The spirits do not want to leave, and you do not want to realize that the pain you feel is caused because of the spirits that have come and taken over the body that only belongs to you.

Humanoids know that you want to keep your thoughts in secret. You think that nobody knows what is going on in your heads. The body is only a grave that you will have to leave behind. For this reason, do not stay in the grave that is not eternal, but instead search for eternity from where you can further develop spiritually. Evil spirits are not like spirits that cannot find peace, they are only searching for a new home because they do not know that they are dead. They do not know what to do. When they come in your body, they just want to continue living. Because of this, you can feel deep depression and troubling crazy thoughts because this other spirit wants you to do what it wants you to do. When you do not know who is who anymore, and you want to get rid of this spirit, begin a prayer which allows you to get a helper from the spirit world who will drive this spirit away from you.

Humanoids create telepathy.

There are many different types of humanoids. There is good and bad telepathy and there are good and bad humanoids. We produce this telepathy, and we want to help you Children of the Earth to understand what it is all about. We produce telepathy only through those who are in such a plane that they are able to be in contact with us. We will return back to Earth when the time is full, and when we do, you will know who was one of us and who was not. This means that many will come and say that they were in contact with us.

Others have free will through the body, but not our own, they live in the future waiting for the time to become full. They know that they cannot change anything through their bodies. They will not become free until after they die. They are prisoners who are buried alive here on Earth. They cannot do what they want because life on Earth, due to the lower self, is not what they hope for. They cannot have fun in the same way as humans. Usually, they just want to spend a lot of time alone searching for God.

We do not always think like you do, Children of the Earth. The future is not what we want. It can never be what we want, but it is what God wants. When we want you to learn that things will become full, you must learn to fulfill them. When you want that time to be full, you have to learn how to live it. When you want all that you want to happen, then you think that you are greater than God is. For this reason, do not be like God is, but be as He would want you to be. When you think that you have a lot of work on Earth you will always come to telepathy with those who never finished their work. You cannot even do anything unless it would be what

God wants. You are not the one who decides everything. You live and you will do what you must, but you do not know what your mission is unless you have made it clear with God first. You want everything that you have to remain, that everything you do not understand to be gone, and that all your thoughts are right. You have to learn how to be silent, and you have to know how to be aware of all the energies around you.

When you come to a time when you were small children, and you lived in the mercy of all the other people, what happened to you then will become trauma for you for the rest of your lives unless you find out what happened to you and why. When you realize how you lived in the mercy of others, you will not want your children to live in your mercy, but instead you learn respect them and help them and no longer try to belittle them. When you do not care about what happened to you, then you do not care about anything anymore, and you live like you are not even alive anymore. When you choose a life where you are no longer alive, you will no longer know how to live, and instead finally you want to die. When you want to die, you can no longer be a part of development, and when you are no longer a part of development, you will die away like a leaf that no longer has anything left to tie it to the tree.

When you have to experience a lot of evil, then learn from evil. When you get a lot of good, then learn from good. When all of your thoughts and your life is tumbled, learn from that so you will better know how to survive. We do not come to you when you want, we are not like an army of the lower self that will step into service when ordered. Men come when we come. We are not tied into time, and we do not allow our lives to be controlled by the lower self like you Children of the Earth.

When you no longer know who is good and who is evil, think of what will make things good and what makes them bad. When you meet people, some good works turn into bad, and things that seem bad turn into good. When you learn that, "Ye shall know them by their fruits," then you will know who is good and who is bad. The Storks did not come here just to whimper like dogs, we came here to do work that has to be completed. When you want to meet us, then do not take those who are not Men. You will meet many humanoids, and many are not what you want them to be, but many of them have something important to tell you, and when you learn what they teach, you might even meet with Men.

Men are in the edge of the heaven, and we are observing your lives. When you no longer know who is who, be patient because nothing that is from God cannot be something that you cannot tolerate.

Humanoids come far from another galaxy, and we have a message of great importance to you Children of the Earth. The future that awaits you is much worse than you can even imagine. When you do not want to change and learn, then nothing can help you. When you want to think that everything you do is only for yourselves, you can never survive into God's Kingdom. In God's Kingdom, there is nobody who only lives to help themselves. Our world will not accept you as you are. You must, through body and spirit, change and be one with God's will so that you may become one of the Children of God's Kingdom.

When you want to learn, and you learn, then you should not be complaining about what you came here to learn, or what you have learned. Do not complain, but instead be happy that you may in the midst of everything else, still continue to learn. There are many that do not have that opportunity anymore, and they only wait to pass, and when they do, they will only be fire, water, earth, and air. They will fall off as the yellow leaves, and they will return after many millions of years, into a new beginning where they may be an animal that will be much smarter than others. In a sense, nothing will ever disappear. Everything that has been created has been created for an eternal life. In fire and Hell burn those that are not able to grow in according to God's Laws. Everything that remains but does not evolve will return back to the beginning. When you meet those who are evil, who no longer have anything good in them, they are Satan's own, and when they go to Satan, they are forced to become a part of Satan who will then take their lives. This is because it is God's will.

God gave Satan an opportunity to become his own ruler, and Satan was granted the power to do as he wanted. He wanted power and he wanted to be even greater than God, that is why he wanted everyone to be his slave, so that they could never be free, and so that they will become a part of him. He will become the master of a body that will rule the darkness. When God said that your time will come full, and you may rule only your own time, he could not complain, but instead he did all that he could. As you know, Satan also serves God, and Satan has his own work on Earth. When his work has come to an end, he will exit and all of his angels will leave with him, and they will be buried for millions of years until it all begins again from the beginning.

When you know what you are here to learn and why, then you have already developed into a higher level. This means that you can no longer make the same mistakes again that you did when you did not know what was going on. When you have learned what you have to, you will come back to the time where you started to wander, (Aka, began reincarnations) and for this reason, you cannot do anything without responsibility anymore. You are responsible for absolutely everything that you do. Your thoughts, your actions, and your choices. There is nothing that you are not responsible for. There is no law that will take away your responsibility for your actions.

When you no longer want to be like others, then do not be like them. Your bodies are like everyone else's, and you live like everyone else, and you want the same things as everyone else. Then why do you want yourself to be different. Do not want, be who you are. You cannot change who you are because of your desires. Be on the Paths of the Four Fires like you are, and as you burn, and as you learn, then you will return. Why do you think that you are alive? You are alive for the sake of learning.

Humanoids create telepathy.

When you think that life is difficult you are not always right. Life is not always as hard as you may think. Your life situations might be difficult, yet you can still develop spiritually and start everything from the beginning. You just need to find the reasons that drove you to difficult life situations. When you have clarified to yourselves why everything came to be as it is, you can start everything again from the beginning.

When you want to stay in the fire of the body's love, then you can never learn serious love. What happened when you fell in love for the first time? No fire burns forever. After the fire burns out, love will begin, and if there was no love, then what was it? When you begin a new relationship on the same grounds as the last, it will not have the same outcome. When you are searching for fire, it can burn you, and when you are searching for love, you may lose it. What is this fire's flame that burns in the body, that forces two people together, whether that was what they wanted or not? This flame is what makes you one with another body, but when you are alone, you can begin to search for a different type of connection. Unless you have something else in common, except the fire that burns in kisses, then maybe you could not have met in any other way. Regardless, there is a reason why something like this happens. Usually, the reason is that karma forces two people together. When you are together, and you live together, the fire begins to fade, and you become familiar with one another.

The body has its own work on Earth, and one of its missions is to reproduce. Once the body finds a suitable partner, it wants to be heard. When the body is granted what it wants it will calm down. When the spirit agrees, then it is ideal to stay together. When the body and the spirit are in an agreement it is also important that the partner is psychologically appropriate. Because of this, it is important to maintain the harmony between the body, soul, and psychology. When you love someone who does not love you, then something is wrong, either in you or in them. Normally, both people agree that they are right for each other. If the relationship is born because of karma, then you cannot change the situations that will occur. When you cannot change or prevent the situations, and you cannot become free, although that is what you want, then the reason for the relationship lies either in karma, or it is psychological. If you want your partner to be different than who they are, you only want to sleep with them. When you want everything to become easier in due time, you have made a wrong choice again. When you want to continue to think about other partners, you are in a completely wrong relationship. When the relationship begins, and you are considering other options, then you are not ready to begin a relationship with the one you are with. When you love, and you are happy, and you do not want anything else but to be alone with this person who you love, you realize that when you go to a place where you cannot be alone, you will leave just to find a place where the two of you can be alone. After the fire has burned out, you can begin to search for each other, and when you get to know each other, you will know if it was love or not. When you have to realize that there never was love, you might learn that the body does not know the love of the spirit. When the body loves and not the spirit, then you are not joyful or happy, but instead you will become angry and are unhappy although you are in love.

After the fire has burned out, and you no longer want to be with your chosen one, although you are still in love you do not want to continue, then you can seek for psychological reasons. After the fire has burned out and you still want to love and you are happy together, and you want to continue to share life together then you have chosen the right partner. When you have bad karma and you fall in love, then you cannot control what happens. You want to end it, but you cannot. You will begin to hate but you cannot stop, and you are unhappy all the time. When you are bewitched and someone has done a love spell, you will be like crazy, and you cannot control yourselves. If the effect is too strong and powerful you can become paranoid and can go mad. When you finally become free, you will never again want to meet this person. You will not know why, but you do not want to see them or know anything about them.

Provided that you have to marry someone like that, the marriage will be short and everything that happens is bad. Nothing will make you happy, not even sex that for the body is mandatory. Also, the body will become paranoid, it will constantly doubt the other body and cannot enjoy sex. When you want nothing like that to happen to you, then be careful with people. When you meet the type of people that do not take your feelings under consideration, stay away from them. Do not play with physical things like appearances, money, or reputation. When you want nobody to want you because of your appearance, money, or your reputation, then do not offer those things when you first meet people. When you want someone to love you, learn how to love first. When you want to learn how to love, then be humble because love is a gift that is given from God, and not a gift that can be stolen.

A-A-A

We read an article about how many had been severely raped as children. Provided that in the future they know what happened to them, they will have many symptoms. One sad but true symptom is multiple personality disorder. What we mean by this is that one personality will shatter and be replaced by other ones. Small children or adults who live independently in order to maintain this terrifying incident. Once the person is able to remember what happened to them, they will feel horrible pain and they may eventually be able to become whole again. This will not always work with everyone, but with many there have been promising results. When you realize that you have such a problem, you need to go to therapy and when you get help you can continue to live your lives again. When something like that has happened, it is the worst thing that can happen in a human's life. This is the worst tragedy that one can think for themselves, yet it is so common that almost everyone has experienced incest, how can this be? What is wrong with a human when they rape their own small children, and after that they can go on living, raping other children for the rest of their lives. It happens all the time. How can telepathy not prevent that from happening? After the child has been raped, they will be in terrible shock, and nobody can see that there is anything wrong. This is something so satanic that you cannot be closer to Satan than when you are with a child rapist. When the child grows up, their life was destroyed because of this. They cannot remember what happened, and consequently they want to destroy themselves in one way or another. Usually, they will also destroy others around them. The results of such filth are so great that the rapist will be condemned straight to hell. Even if they had been victims in their own childhood. What has gone wrong with a human when they do not believe in God anymore, or in Satan? They live their lives as it would be judgment day on Earth. They do as much evil as they can before they die. They do not care about the consequences, not even the ones they will have in this life. If they would care, they would not do what they do. Because Satan has gotten power over humans, persecution of the Christians will begin. Each one who remains pure will be under persecution. This means that anyone with any spiritual development will be persecuted. Provided that this has happened to you, come back to God and trust God, allow God to guide all things in your lives. This is a difficult time for all of those that are pure, but do not let go of faith because God knows everything that has happened to you and will make sure everyone who has caused you suffering will get what they deserve. Whatever happens, God will know what happened.

We do not come because of anything that comes through the lower self. The body that you have is a body that Satan gave you with a lower self that is from Satan. God created the spirit, not the body. This body that you carry is from Satan, not from God. When God gave you a body, it was light and translucent. You have a body that has its own will and its own temptations. When you become a prisoner of your own body, you will also be imprisoned by Satan, who gave the body his own spirit, the low spirit. This low spirit is the reason that you want to do evil things to yourselves and others.

When God created a human, He created a human in His own image. He is the spirit, and you have a spirit. When Satan created a human, he created it to be such that it would be subject to the laws of the Earth, not the laws of the spirit. When you want to be reborn and be in the spirit, in a sense, you will have to find the spirit that is in you, and you will overcome the body that you have. This is why you do not know yourselves, do you not you know that the body is subject to its own laws, and that you are subject to your laws. As we have previously explained, you have to take control over your own bodies and your low selves, you have to rule these energies. When you become free from the low spirit, and free from your own body, then you will defeat the low spirit. When you have defeated the low spirit and the body, then you have defeated Satan.

Other beings that come and teach you are others that come from another star. Some of them are evil, and some are good like we are. There are many of us in space, and we all have our own laws. When you do not know your own laws, then you have to leave your only mind, which is the thought world of the body and learn how to face things only in spirit. When you learn the thought world of the spirit, you can experience new things and discover a life that is subject to different laws. When you do not know the purpose of life, and you doubt everything that you have heard, and you think that life is just a coincidence that you became a part of, life is not a coincidence, but a problem that God and Satan solve by helping humans into flesh and bone. This life on Earth is a battle between the spirit and low spirit, and both of these spirits live in the same space, which is the body.

When you leave your body, you will enter another space where you will continue to learn, after this space has been passed, you will move into another and then yet another. Nothing will stop this process that will help you to learn even more. After you have learned enough, then you can return and start everything again from the beginning. If you were evil, you will get difficulties that you can learn from, and if you were good and you helped, you will help more and teach others. Do not ever underestimate what you are living through. What you live through is what you will learn.

Each one has their own, even those who do not know how to love. When you learn that love is never what you want, you will learn that you need to learn how to love. When you want love, you will receive love, but do you know how to love right, and is this love ever what you wanted? You cannot want love only to fulfill all of your dreams. Whatever you want, you will get, but do you know how to want things that are good for you? Usually, you want things that will only destroy you. For this reason, you have to learn to know what you want, so that you do not cause pain to yourselves just because of something that you wanted. When you become free of your mind, your low self, and your body, then you will be free. When you are free, you will not want things that only cause pain anymore.

When you learn, then teach others. When you love, then love. Your body which through you love is not the spirit. You can only love through the spirit, never through the body or the low spirit. That will never be love, only selfishness, which will always cause pain. Spiritual love is never selfish, and it is real. It will never wound the other, only heal, and spiritual love will help you grow, and spiritual love will always sacrifice and will never ask for a sacrifice. If you want to love in the spirit then overcome the lower self, the body, and your mind and come to the spirit that is in you. When the lower self no longer controls you then you can learn about love. Love is not what you want, it just is, and as the love grows so will you grow with it. You cannot change things that you have through your new body. Others will have a better body and others will always have more than you do, but you can grow in spirit and become happy. Only those who live in spirit can be happy. Nobody can reach happiness through the body, the low self, or the mind, only through the spirit that remains and does not change. The beginning of everything was the spirit, and the end of everything is the spirit. This is what you will learn, and this is what you want to learn.

We do not always talk in this way. We can also come and speak through people if we want to. We will never leave you Children of the Earth. We will always come back and help you. How can we leave you if you have the spirit that God gave you? The spirit that you have is the same spirit that is in us. Men will never leave you. We will always come back when the time is full. Humanoids always have free will to choose what they want to do. Men want to come and speak to you when you want to know. We will come and tell you what you need to learn. When you think that someone else is better than the other, then you do not think right. All the Children of God are equal, one has just had more difficulties than the other, but the spirit that you have has originated from the same God. When you want yourself to be more than others, do not think that Men think with their bodies. We think in spirit and the spirit guides our thoughts. When you choose wrong, and you make wrong choices, you have been controlled by the low spirit. For this reason, do not allow your low spirit to lead you so that you do not have to regret.

Children of the Earth, when the time is full, Men will come. We cannot unless that is what you want. Men are on the edge of the heaven. You cannot come to Men unless that is what we want. How could you come with Men unless that that is what you wanted? When the time comes full, we come. The Kingdom of God is so grand that each one has their own place. How can anyone be without a place when God has created everything? At night, when you think about what has happened to you, leave your bodies, and go where your home is. When you can leave your own body, then why are you sad about what has happened to you. You can learn about your time on Earth, and when you no longer need learning you will leave. When you do not have the strength to bear all the evil, during your sleep go where you are safe. When you pray that you can have peace, you do not understand that there is no peace on Earth. To have peace you have to leave. Your body cannot go with you, and if you do not want to leave without your body then you cannot go.

Children of Earth, when you have encountered too much evil, you have to think about what evil is. When you realize that there is evil everywhere, and you can no longer believe in good, believe in who you are. Be good, help people, and show that good exists and that evil cannot take hold of you through the lower self. When you have learned from evil, you can teach about good. How can you teach about good if you do not know evil? Nothing that comes from the higher self is from the lower self. That is what you are learning here on Earth.

When you realize that life is a lesson, then you have learned what you must. What is evil's reward? It is that it will die. The reward of evil is death. And the evil knows that, it knows what its reward is. That is why the evil will not stop until it has done all the evil it can, and it can never stop until it dies. That is why, whatever has happened to you, you have defeated Satan, and when you have defeated Satan, you will become free and you can live. When you have a lot of bad memories, try to gather good new memories, and think about what you can do when you can control nature's laws. When you have defeated Satan, as a gift you will receive abilities that you did not have before. Once you learn how to use these abilities, then you can help, heal, and change things. When you want to leave Earth, remember that life is a gift from God, and when you received this gift you received an opportunity to become better than what you were in your past life. As you develop, you can return back to the source where you came from. There is a home in Heaven for each one who wants to come back. Each one has a place where they can come. Sometimes the body is just powerless when there are so many problems on Earth. That is why you need to take good care of the body. You can feed it well and allow it to rest. The body is not guilty for those things that have happened to it.

Humanoids produce telepathy.

When you come to the edge of heaven and meet with Men, you do not remember it. When you sleep and wake up, you will only remember the dreams that the body had. The dreams of the body are different than the spirit. When you learn to control your dreams, you can through your body remember where you were. When you learn to control energies, you will learn that evil always respects God, although you cannot understand it. Why do you always complain that the world is evil? You can be different. You can be the good, and you can help people who do not know what Heaven or what Hell is. You came on Earth to help. When you want to control energies, then you have to defeat Satan, and when you want for everything to be good, then pray that God will help you so that everything will be good. When you do not know your own body, and you do not know your spirit, how can you do anything that would be right? When you learn what you have, then you can leave the bad times behind you, and start everything from the beginning. Wherever you will go, you will be doing work that God has given you.

Children of the Earth,

You do not think about things enough to know what is going on here on Earth. You just live and die, and you never stop to think about what this is all about. When you die, it is too late to think about what everything was about. You have to think about things when you are alive, and when you live you have to learn and know what happens and why. When a lot of bad things happen, you still do not know what this is all about. You just live like nothing would have ever happened, and when you die, you do not even know if you were good or evil or what you were, and when Satan comes and gets his own, you do not even know that you are his own. While you are alive, find out who you are, and when you no longer want to be Satan's own, then make amends to become better. When you want to be good, that is not enough, you have to defeat Satan to know whether you are good or evil. When you have defeated Satan, then you will not doubt anymore who you will choose, but you will always know who was your worst enemy.

Many come onto Earth, and they want to help. They want to develop, and they want to learn. When they are here, they lose everything that they wanted before they were born. When they die, they can no longer do what they were supposed to do through their bodies. Why don't you awaken before it is too late? When you are no longer alive, it is too late. You cannot do without a body what you can do through your body. (We do not come unless you want. We mean if you Lea, do not want to receive Men, we do not come. We do not force you to telepathy like evil spirits when they come. They force Lea and they want to take Lea's life.)

Crazy is the one who wants to become famous because they know how to use evil energy. Each one who does will become a prisoner of their own karma. They also have to carry the responsibilities of what they have done to others, not just to themselves. Nothing will change karma even if there were all kinds of reasons why the person became evil. Nothing changes karma. Karma will always remain the same, no matter how many bad things have happened. Humans can always choose from good or evil. Even though children are pure, and they do not know about evil, and they want to love everyone, and they know how to love, even they are under the laws of karma. They live through things that were wrong in their past life, and this is how they also participate in the laws of karma at a very early age. When a lot of evil is being done to children, the ones doing the evil are also doing it to their own childhoods. Unless the adults want to change the child's destiny, the same destiny as the child's will be waiting for them.

When we read an article from a magazine that talked about incest, and we realized how much incest there is on Earth. We concluded that each one who had lived the fate of incest as a child had a terrible desire to have children of their own. They often want to have children that will have the same fate, and why do they do that? Men think that maybe, first there is a lot of pain, and then after that even more pain, and after that even more. There is no other explanation other than that the first pain forces them to cause even more pain, and then that pain into even worse pain. That is why when you realize that you have a lot of pain, take care of it so that you will not get more pain, or cause pain to others. When you cannot get help, even when you try, it is because of bad karma, and that the people near you are evil. When there is nothing you can do, stay patient because maybe in due time you will get mercy. Provided that you want to help others, do that so you can receive help for yourselves. Whatever your life situation is, it should always remain open to helping others. Nobody can say that everything was so bad back then that they could not have helped. When your life returns back to good, it might be too late for the one you were supposed to help.

When you come to a time when you do not have the strength to believe in God, and you have lost all your hope, do not abandon God even then. Even if you do not believe in God at that moment, God has not disappeared. When you abandon God, then you accept Satan, and once you accept Satan, you will no longer survive. When you feel that God is absent, just wait so that there will be a better time where you can meet Him again. When you abandon Him by saying that He does not exist, that everything is evil, and that the time for all miracles is over, you have simply come to a point where you are just too tired from all the evil that you have encountered. This will pass once your life situation gets better. Sometimes you have to want bad things so that the karma can begin. This means that unless you want bad things, then you can never pay the karma that you have. The bad things teach you about pain and about yourselves, and this is how in the end you will find out what you really are. When you have survived all the evil, you will know what you are, and also know how to appreciate yourselves. The spirit world is always near you. The good and evil spirits want to take their own. How can you know whether you are good or an evil spirit unless you have a lot of tribulations? After you have survived these tribulations, you will know who you are, and you can have peace when you die when your time is full. When an evil spirit dies, Satan will come and take them to Hell. Such a death is horrible. They can never again make any changes to their lives.

When you want to do things right be careful with everything that you do, and when you want to know what God's will is, and what Satan's will is, then do what you think is right and not what you want. You have a desire to all that is evil, that is within each one of you, it is a gift you have received from Satan. You have to conquer your desire to do evil and to cause harm, and when you can do that you have conquered Satan. Provided that you are a victim of severe psychological trauma, and you have compulsions to do bad things against your own will, go and find help immediately. If you do not seek help, then you will be responsible for your actions.

When you have lost your sanity and there are evil spirits in you, and problems that you can no longer control, you will need the help of others. If nobody helps you then they will have to pay the karma for that. When you have gone mad and you kill and do something like that, without any knowledge of what your actions are, you will face karma to help everyone who is on the verge of losing their mind.

When you learn that there is life on multiple different planes, and when you learn to live on these planes you will grow spiritually. All difficult life situations will open new dimensions in a human, unless they desire to open the dimensions of the lower self that exists nearly as many. Now that you know you have many choices, make them consciously so that you will no longer choose wrong. When you want the world to change, then change yourselves. That will be the first step, that the whole world will open its eyes and change. When one day you can no longer choose, but instead your destiny has been sealed, everything will be too late. That is why, do what you can because maybe you will not have a tomorrow and your time has come to full.

Men explain telepathy to Lea.

We come from a far, from another star and we want to leave a message from outer space to the Children of the Earth. There is a lot of harm and suffering here on Earth that everyone knows about. We will explain why things are the way they are. There, on the other side of the heavens there is no lower self that causes so many problems to the Child of the Earth. The lower self drives a human to evil and suffering. Each one can find this cruel and evil dark side of themselves. Children of Earth are also given another side to themselves so that they can conquer Satan and become a Child of God. When you have defeated the low self within you, then you have defeated Satan. When the low self has been defeated, you will be as pure as Jesus Christ. Although, as you know, this is not an easy mission. You can be good and live like other people and still be evil. When finally you will be in temptation, your dark side will surface and take over you. This is why you cannot know whether you are good or evil unless you are tempted. Only a temptation will finally show you what kind of person you really are. When you want to develop spiritually and become good, you will go to church, and you will stop doing all evil. Now that you think that you are good, you will realize that you do not know anything about yourselves. You do everything as you should, yet you do not know what you are because everything that you do, you do because someone else said so. When you really want to become good, all you can do is hope that you will be given a very difficult life. This is the only path for you to finally know who you really are. When you are given a difficult life, you will learn many things about yourselves, and through this, you will know whether you are a good or an evil person. When there is a lot of evil, you may become broken. This happens to many. Many people will break and become a part of themselves, they are no longer one but many together. When this happens, all of your parts will be tearing you in different directions and you will be left with your spirit that can hold you together. When the spirit is strong it can hold you together no matter how many small parts you are in.

When you have to be in between Heaven and Hell, you will learn that Hell exists and Heaven exists, and when you have to live without light, you will learn that the light is, and when you learn to live without God, you will learn that God is. When you have to live without love, you will learn that love is. When you learn to live without a friend, you will learn that life is, and finally also friends. When you learn to live through your greatest pain alone, you will learn that you are strong and powerful, and when you cannot find anyone to love you, then you will learn how to love yourselves, and by helping others you will be helped. Humanoids teach you so that you can learn how to live consciously and so that you can learn what life is.

When you want yourself to be a humanoid, then learn first how to be a human, and once you have learned how to be a human, you will no longer care what you are. You are God's creation, and you have a reason to be fighters for your own lives. You have to fight for the sake of your own lives so that you can be alive. For this reason, it is not of importance who you are, but it is important that you are.

When you love God, then you also love yourselves right. This is the most important lesson you have to learn, because God gave you a spirit, and your spirit is a part of God, you need to love the spirit that resides in you and in this way, you also love God. When God gave you the spirit, He gave it to you as a gift, and He wanted you to appreciate this gift. When He wants you to liberate your spirit from evil and help it back into the light, then He will give you many things so that you can learn what evil is, and what good is. For this reason, even though bad things happen to you, you must always think that God is good. After the evil is gone, all that will remain is good, and after that you will know why all the bad things that happened to you happened. This is mercy by which you can enlighten your own spirit and you can be sure of who you are. You are God's Children and that you will learn what you have to, and when you learn to be thankful of the evil that you have overcome, then you have conquered it.

This was written by Cirius.

Men leave.

Men are here.

We do not live like you, Children of the Earth. We do not harm others and we do not want you to think that we begin this only so that we can be in contact. We begin this so that we can teach you and everyone else through you. When we come, we only come to teach. When you want us to come, we do not, we come when the time is full. For this reason, you will realize that the time on a flying craft is different than yours. You will finally realize that although you come to Earth to learn things, you cannot learn unless you want to make big changes in yourselves. Yet, you cannot change unless you want to learn, and when you do want to learn, and yet you continue to do the same things, we cannot influence your wandering. When you want to learn, then you must change, and when through the body you change, you can no longer be as you were in your past life. When you no longer can be as you used to be, then you want to be different, and through that you will learn new things.

When you have learned from life, then you can learn from the spirit. When you learn from the spirit, you no longer care about who you are or how your body is, but instead you want to be in the spirit, not in the body that will be taken away from you. When you learn that you and the body are not as you wish, then you know that you are receiving telepathy from your body. This means that if you are not in harmony with yourselves, then there are spirits in you, or you are in Satan's telepathy. For this reason, drive away the evil that is possessing you, and start everything from the beginning so that you can live in harmony within yourselves. You do not exist through the body, but you exist because of the spirit, and the spirit does not care what kind of body it has. It does not care whether it is a man or woman, nor does it care if it is beautiful or ugly. The spirit lives in the body and it wants to express what it has to. The spirit wants to learn, and it wants the body to obey its will, and it wants itself to be clean and free. The spirit does not want to be a prisoner in its own body. When the spirit is being held prisoner, it wants to escape. It wants to go away and leave the body. When the evil spirits come and take over the body, the spirit will escape, and if the spirit stays to fight, it will go through severe pain and agony that it cannot escape. For this reason, you have to keep your body clean from the evil spirits. The evil spirit also causes your spirit to hope that the body is better, younger, and stronger so that it can drive away the evil spirit.

When you want your body to no longer take in an evil spirit, you must win the body's trust. You have to teach your body to fight against the spirit world which is always ready to move in. Many spirits wander not knowing where to go, they are always searching for a new home because they do not know how to be without a body. They wander from place to place and usually come into a body that has a black hole. This black hole has been created because of some trauma, and when the human prays, this black hole will be filled with light. When they are angry, this hole will become large and black again, and the evil spirit can enter. When the human is depressed, this hole will become gray, and once again evil energies are able to enter. Once the spirit has entered, it wants the body that it took possession of to be different because its own body used to be different before it died. Usually, the spirit can cause the person who resides to become different, to look different, or be a different sex, and if the spirit is strong, it will fully take possession of the body.

Humanoids produce telepathy.

Men have been in contact with Lea many times through her body. When we come, we come from Lea's light and not from a black hole. We only come if we have a message and we will say what we need to say. When we come and talk, we do not want even one word to go without being heard, and we want everything that we say to be remembered. For this reason, be ready so that when we do come, we will not come in vain. When you receive this brother's message, then come and make amends to become better. As you are given yet another opportunity, you may still fall. When you fall and you do not know what to do, pray for God to send you a helper. When you are given a helper, learn what you are being taught and change.

When you have had a difficult life, and there are spirits in you, maybe you are here to learn about these difficulties. You will realize that what you deserve is what you will receive. Short is a life on Earth, and it is short so that you have the strength to live it. When you have developed enough, then you can enter other spiritual planes and your life will be much longer.

God in His mercy gave you a short life so that you will have the strength to live it. When the time is full, you will leave, and when the time is full, you will come back until you are allowed to go where life is better than what it is on Earth.

There is a lot of evil and a lot of pain here and you yourselves create even more pain to each other. You can only feel your own pain but not the one of another. When you think that you are the only one who feels pain, you are just beginning a path of learning where others also have that pain, and that you have no right to create more pain, but instead you should lessen their pain.

You cannot be alone when everyone you know is as lonely as you. You will learn that there is no loneliness, there is only a path that takes you to God, or a path that takes you away from God.

Everyone who chooses the wrong path will be lonely, and those who are on God's path are never alone. When you realize that what you are living through is your what you have chosen, then you can no longer harvest hatred. You harvest hatred because you do not know how to love, and when you do not know how to love, then you can never have serious love.

When you cannot receive love, then you cannot learn, and when you cannot learn, you will go to Satan who will take you in the end. When you want to learn and you do not learn, do not think that God has abandoned you, but think instead that what you get is what you deserve. When you get what you deserve, you will finally learn, maybe not today, but maybe in your next life, and when that happens, then you will understand.

We do not want you to think that Men are beings from the lower planes. We were angels and now we are Men who live in flying craft. We were angels who you wanted to meet, and now we are that no longer because we came closer to you Children of the Earth. When you want to know who Men are, you will meet with those who have met us. When you want us to come, we can allow ourselves to be seen if it is necessary, but normally it is not what we want because we want you to learn in spirit so that you are not awake only through your body but awake in spirit. When we come, we will always bring forth a brother's message from the edge of the heavens. This message is always a lesson that we want to give. When you meet us, you will no longer think as you used to, and we do not want you to change for the sake of us, but the for the sake of yourselves. When you meet other humanoids, who through the body and spirit are different, then you can learn about the differences of which you can learn to respect. You can learn about everything that happens to you and when you learn you will become better. You can develop spiritually. When you do not want to learn, and you are afraid of new life and death, and the Storks, and everything that happens to you, then you cannot develop.

Do not be afraid but be ready for everything. Be ready to change, be ready to die, and be ready to love. When time is full you must be ready. Maybe there will not be another chance, and if you are not ready you will come to a state that you can no longer escape. Nothing can save someone who does not want to develop spiritually. Nobody else can help someone who does not want to be helped. When you meet many people who want something from you, then give them spiritual teachings. When you meet people who are in distress, then help them if you can. When you meet people who want your love, then love them. Love them like you love your brother. When you want love and you do not receive it, then pray for God to love you. When He loves you, then you will no longer need love like you did before. Nobody else can love you like God, who has loved you so much that He gave you a spirit that can grow towards the light that will never diminish.

When you want for all things to be different than what they are now, then be patient and maybe when you wake up, they will be different already. When you wake up, you will realize that the only thing that needs to change is you. When you change, then the things around you will change as well. Do not leave anyone who cannot live without you. When you are the only one for someone, then do not leave them behind. You have to find someone else who can help them so that they can survive without you. When you leave people who cannot live without you, then you have done a bad deed against God.

When God said, "There is no emptiness without pain", He meant that everything that is alive can experience pain and anguish. If you cannot understand that, then you have not learned anything. When you no longer have the strength to help someone who is causing you pain, then you have to leave them. They also need to realize that they do not have the right to cause pain to anyone, but do not leave the ones who do not want to harm you, and who depend on you, like children, the elderly, your wives, or the ones who are pregnant. Do not leave the ones who are in deep distress, like the ones who have a lot of problems, like the ones who do not know how to live, like the ones that are weak, and the ones whose only good is you. Do not leave them so that they can at least have that love which is meant for them, you are meant to love them. When you are searching for love, then learn to love. You will be given another opportunity. You cannot look for love if there is no love in you.

Men come from the edge of the heavens to explain life.

Children of the Earth, when you do not have the strength to live on this planet, and you want to die, first come to back to the Heavenly Father and die after that. If you die before you have encountered God, then you cannot encounter Him after you die. Behind the new helper, are the other helpers. Some come from another planet, some come from heaven, and some come from the beginning of the new time. Humanoids want to help you. Familiar thoughts are familiar and strange thoughts are strange. When you encounter strange thoughts, maybe you are meeting someone who is not from the Earth. When you want to become good and change, then take yourselves by the hand and go back into your childhoods and ask yourselves, what made you evil?

We read an article about a girl who killed herself and her children. After she had died, everyone said that she was evil. When we read the story, we became very sad that someone who had small children wanted to die. She did not have anyone who wanted to help her when she had difficulties. She did not have anyone who would have loved her or cared about her when she had a hard time. Then why did people say that she was evil? Why didn't anybody say that she was lonely and unhappy, and that everyone around her was evil? Humans are evil, and when those who want to be good like children, others will come and do evil to them so that they will become evil as well. The nature of human's evilness is old and deep. Originally, the human was not good but evil, and because of that you cannot be Children of God, but you are Children of Satan. Provided that God sends a Child of God to Earth, Satan will attack them even more fiercely, and when they cannot bare their lives anymore, they will kill themselves. When that happens, you will have to carry the responsibility for their death. Many Children of God have killed themselves because they did not have the strength to live among the Children of Satan. Like I said, it is Satan's work what happens to them. Many who have lived a difficult life are tired. They came here to help but were not capable because Satan made their life so difficult. God does not want to give a difficult life to anyone. It is Satan's will what happens to the Children of God. When you came here to help, and you wanted to bring light, Satan and his troops took your life and began destruction.

That is why Men came from the flying crafts to help because you are Children of God.

When Men come, Satan will step aside, and when we come, the evil will be gone. When we come, the time will be full, and when we come you will get what belongs to you. When the evil gets what belongs to it, then the good will get what belongs to good. When the time is full it will happen, and Satan and his army will go back to where it came from, and everyone who is a Child of God will come back to God's Kingdom. When you do not know any more about who is good and who is evil, then you no longer know who you are, and when you do not know who you are, you no longer know what is what. This means that you have had so much evil happen to you that you no longer know what is what. When you find the truth, you will know what this is about. Whatever happens to you, do not care, because what has happened, has already happened, and what has not happened does not exist.

When you chose a life on Earth, you have chosen a lot of pain. There is a lot of pain here, and you must overcome that pain. That pain is what will purify. The pain is a fire starter that will help you to open your light. It will also teach you about what Satan is, and there are many who help Satan. Do not be one of them, because each one who is on Satan's side has already been condemned to Hell, and Hell is not a place on Earth, but it is a place much worse than Earth, where there is endless pain and there is no hope. Each inhabitant of Hell is like the future that is waiting for the Earth, with no hope, without love, and without anything other than their own evil that will never leave them. You, who are of God, have freedom, love, and happiness. You can always share the love that will never disappear. When you choose evil, you will have to pay its price. Once you have paid it you are free to come back to God. Each one who nowadays is innocent to their fate will inherit gifts that others do not have. Only a victim can receive gifts, not the ones with bad karma.

Humanoids come and want to announce through telepathy that everything that you have suffered is written in God's book, and when the time has come full, everyone will have to pay for causing suffering that was not meant for you. That is why, be patient and wait for everything that is meant for you to be given to you. Work on Earth is painful, but it will reward you more than you know when it is all over. When you become free from Satan you will receive a lot of power with which you can always defeat Satan again. You can always come, help, and always drive Satan away when you want. That is why it is important to defeat Satan, and once you have done that you will be as pure as Jesus Christ.

This was sent by Adam, and many greetings to everyone.

Men produce telepathy.

Sometimes psychics are evil, and the telepathy that they produce comes from Satan. Sometimes, they do not even know this, and sometimes they do. They are mean and evil, and they openly do black magic, etc., they produce telepathy through their mind and body instead of the spirit. They want for everything they say to come true. They want to create thoughts and give birth to the Earth with their abilities. These are called black magicians. Similar to them are all of those who take control of other people who follow them. They want to be able to control everything that happens. Such control is satanic. This also happens within families and relationships, where one wants to control the other one's life. This is Satan worship. Nobody is allowed to control anyone else's life. Human beings are meant to be free to make their own decisions and resolutions. Whatever they want, that is their will, and they are responsible for their actions only to God. They will also have to settle up with Satan when their time comes. When you want to do everything right, then do not cause suffering to other people.

Everyone who wants to help and has helped, has also helped themselves for a better life. When you want to help others, then you have learned something. When you want someone to help you, you will always meet someone who will help you. When you have learned that life is a school that you are participating in, you will learn each day what you came here to learn. When you want the world to not be evil, then stop being evil. When you want to be loved, then begin to love. When you want to be able to learn what you have to do, then learn what you can. When you cannot learn anymore, then you do not have more to learn. Because of this, be willing and open to know and feel the life near you so that you will know who you are and what you came here on Earth to learn. If you do not know what your mission is, or why you exist, then you can look at everything that has happened to you and maybe that will teach you what you came here to learn. When you learn to accept life as it is, then you have learned many things. You cannot change things, you can only change yourselves. You cannot change others, you can only learn about things that you do not understand. You cannot prevent things from happening and you cannot always begin things that are not meant for you. When you want changes, changes will come when it is their time. You cannot with your spirit or your body, change something that is in your destiny.

When you want to love or fall in love, it will happen to you when it is time. Love has its own laws, and your ideas or fears cannot prevent these laws from fulfilling. When serious love comes into your lives, you will be ready because you will know that your time is full. When serious love comes to you, you want to be theirs and you do not doubt. When you think that you are difficult, you will become easy. When you think that you are different, will you become the same. When you want to make love, you will become love, and when the time has come full, serious love will come into your lives. Provided that you fall in love like the wind, and you do not know where you are going to, or what you are doing, then you have fallen in satanic love. Love like this will make people paranoid and they think that anyone else is better than themselves. They think that anyone can take their loved one away. This type of love is from Satan. Love given from God is different. The threat that was in control before is gone and the person can be in peace knowing that their loved one is safe and not scary, they know that they do not want to cause pain or harm them.

Men are here producing telepathy.

When you want to know about love, and what is right and what is wrong, you will learn that life is complicated and difficult. Nobody will survive without making mistakes and wrong choices. Everyone will make wrong choices and mistakes, and when you have learned this, you have already learned a lot. Provided that you want to know what a soulmate is, we can explain this. Soulmates are in a way, one and the same soul that have gone into spiritual development as two. This means that the soul is the same but in two different humans. This type of couple is rare, but they do exist. If you meet your soulmate, you can be sure that they are the same as you are. You will not doubt it for a moment, but instead you will know that this other one is a part of your future and a part of the past that you have already lived. Everyone has been given their soulmate, and some also had to lose them. That is why some are so very lonely and can never be happy with anyone. Soulmates are always connected to each other, no matter how different the life circumstances they are in. They can live in the opposite sides of the Earth, they can be different in age, it can be that the other one is dead and the other alive, or the other one can live in a different star living another life.

When soulmates are allowed to meet, they will always love each other no matter how big their differences are. This kind of love is different. These people are very much in love, and spiritually in love with one another. They support each other and help each other to live better and become happy. They will usually help other people as well because together they have more power than otherwise. When the soulmates are allowed to encounter each other, it is usually when they are ready to meet. This will usually happen when they want to meet, and they have completed everything they had to do before meeting each other. When you meet your soulmate, you will know that they are the one who is a part of you. You will not doubt, but instead you will be sure, and you will be ready. Sometimes, such an encounter will happen in the wrong time and they want to be separated from each other until they are ready to continue the relationship. This only happens for a few. Usually, they cannot meet during the same life so that they can better develop spiritually, and when they do meet, they are already highly spiritually developed, and they are willing to help with the power that they receive from each other. This power is the kind that only soulmates can get. Together they are double, and their mission is normally to heal, help, and give information to people. Nobody has to look for their soul mate because they will meet when the time has come full. Other couples learn from each other. They learn to love difference and different kinds of people. When they separate, if this has been the right spiritual development, they have developed greater spiritually.

When the relationship is karma, things cannot be created. They will just happen whether these two want that or not. When the relationship is satanic, it just creates a lot of suffering, and the couple will finally end up hating each other. They only want to hurt each other. When you want to develop in a relationship, and you do not have one, learn that what comes to you is meant for you.

Provided that you still think of yourselves as ignorant and weak, then do not change anything that you are not familiar with. If you have doubts, and you are afraid, then remain living as you currently do until you have a certainty of what you need to do. Do not force yourselves to do anything that you doubt because often you have an intuition that is warning you. When you learn to listen to this intuition, you might be able to take better care of your life. As you learn to take better care of your life then you will learn to love yourself.

There have been many writings about the beginning of the new age, which will happen when people can no longer stand their own evilness. Through body and soul they want to change. Through body, they will learn when many have died, and through the soul when they are in constant suffering doing what they want but nothing can ease the pain. There are many who only want to die, and many who cannot feel any joy or happiness through their body. No matter what they do the bad feelings only grow. For this reason, humans will finally want to change, and they will change everything that they can so that they can rest in peace when they die. When they have learned their lessons, they will change, but the time will not come without redemption. This redemption will cause a lot of suffering that cannot be prevented.

When a husband leaves his wife and children for a new woman, he will have glory because of the new wife, but no one will help the woman whom the husband left. All of man's evil deeds will be divided in two parts. Many will be seeking for relief from a street girl and get aids which they will bring home to their wives and children. Many will leave their families to be able to get a new wife without children so that she can better serve him. Many men will also want sons so that they can give their son a new opportunity to be a man who wants a wife who can be left to his mercy. When all the evil that has to happen has happened, then will come the antichrist, who will take his own and will finally go back to hell with his own. After that, the new age will come.

The new age will be built by those who were left on Earth. By this time so much evil has happened that those people who are left are the last people on Earth, and there will not be many of them. Many will bring secrets to publicity, and many want to be the brothers and daughters of the Earth and do not want through their body or their spirit to create any more suffering that has already happened. This new time will have a thousand years of the Great White Brotherhood of light's Kingdom, *(* The Great White Brotherhood also known as the Great Brotherhood of Light or the Spiritual Hierarchy of Earth, is perceived as a Spiritual organization composed of those Ascended Masters who have risen from Earth into immorality but still maintain an active watch over the world… etc. Wikipedia.) which has helped bring forth this work. They will be behind this development, and they will produce a lot of help. When humans are finally ready to be worth their life. Because of all this, nobody who is evil can be good. Angels are never evil and nobody who is evil can be good. The good is good and the evil is evil. Therefore, it does not matter what has happened to the human before, nobody who is good wants to do evil, and no evil wants to do good, no matter what their circumstances were.

All this was given to Lea by Adam from the edge of heaven.

Men want to leave a message to Lea.

This comes through body and soul, and through this the brothers can begin contact.

This is Adam.

You will not get to meet your soulmate in this lifetime because it is I. If you want, we have always been in contact with each other and I will say this so that you will know that it is I, Adam, who lives in a flying craft. You receive telepathy because you are telepathic and can receive this. You can also be in touch with the spirit world but be careful because any spirit can come and take over your body. Pray when you begin telepathy, so that your spiritual level is higher. There are many spirits here not just one but many. When you want to know about future, you can use the spirit world, through the body what will happened cannot be explained. You can use spirit world only when the spirits are in the light, dark spirits don't know about the future and will misinform. When you want correct information, you can pray to God for help and He will guide you through the information you need.

A-A-A

Life is short because time is short, and when the time comes the work will be done. When there is still a lot work left to do, you will have to finish all that you have to do. When you are old, and you have no more strength left to do anything, then you have finished your work. When you live without any calling, something has gone wrong in your lives. Everyone has a lot of work that has to be finished. When you live, get weak, and you lose all of your abilities, then something with your development has gone wrong. God's purpose is not so that the human will become weak, incapable and be a living dead, even when old, the human can do the work they were born to do that they did not have time to complete when they were young and strong. When you do not know what your mission is in life, or what it should have been, then you do not know why you are alive. You have abandoned the purpose of life. You do not know what spiritual development is, what life is, what death is, and when you do die, you will not know where you are going or who you are, and you do not know anything about anything. Perhaps the lamp that was burning inside you, burned out.

Humanoids gave this telepathy to Lea.

A-A-A

Although you have had a difficult time, and a lot of evil has happened to you, you are still whole, and you did not become evil. This is what God wanted. He just wants to know who will become evil, and who will not. Although you come into this life in a way where there is no evil in you and there is no beauty or ugliness in you, you know how to be happy and sad and you only have the awareness that there is light and there is darkness. You come on to Earth with the knowledge that there is light, and that there is darkness. You spend a lot of time in the light when you are babies, you are like angels are, but you are not angels, you are human beings, and you know that you are not angels. You will begin life where you learn about telepathy and from telepathy you learn about evil. When you cannot speak, you will learn telepathy, when you meet evil, you will learn from evil, and when you trust in God, you will learn from good because you will never have anything else but God, and what else could be given to you.

When your life ends, you will come to two places, one is Heaven, Heaven is Heaven and the other one is similar to the place that you come to before you die and before you are born. You will first come here, and you will find out what you have to do only if you want. When you do not want to know, you will have to stay here, you can choose what to do. If you want to stay, you will become ghosts, and when you no longer want to be ghosts, you can continue on to the second plane where you can meet friends, loved ones, and also enemies who you cannot have peace from, but you cannot do much here. You can only try to live a regular life which is not always so successful. Some meet others in this plane, some will continue to live together, and some just pass by like in life.

When you invite bad friends into your home, you will be in a bad mood. When you meet evil people, you cannot always run away, but sometimes you have to stay near them, and they can cause severe damage to your aura body. Evil always causes color damage to your aura body because their own aura is shattered. When your aura body becomes damaged, all you can do is pray and try to be alone as much as you can so that you can have time to heal your aura body. If you feel that you are not healing, all you can do is allow time to pass by. All wounds, even the ones that feel like they cannot be healed will be healed. When you meet evil, you will know because you do not feel good around them. Even the ones that seem good, you just want to avoid them and you just stay away from them. If you fall in love with an evil person, you have fallen into an evil telepathy that is, in a sense, hypnosis. Evil people can hypnotize to be able to get people under their control. They know how to do this because they use energies that good people do not use. These energies are Satan's worship energies and come directly from Satan. They are aware of this. When you are in the control of an evil person all you can do is fight against it and learn how to protect yourselves. When you are not sure who is good, and who is evil, you will soon realize that no one who is good wants to hurt anyone. Only evil hurts. Each one has to decide for themselves who is good and who is evil, nobody else can help you to know. Each one is here to learn, even the evil ones, they might have just this life left to try to become good.

Humanoids are here. We come from the edge of the heavens, and we want to help you become better and learn to understand life. When you want to escape life and you want to die, there will be a new body waiting. Nobody can leave their life with their own will. When God has said that everything has its time, He means that each one will have their time, and it is not a human's choice to determine how long that time is. Sometimes it is short, and sometimes it is long.

A-A-A

Many are old souls, and they are either good or bad. They will cause a lot of suffering if they are evil, and if they are good, they are very good. If they want to help, they will really do that. Many are only here to do work in this life. They do not even search for anything themselves. They will do what they have to, and they will leave when they have to. However, beware of the evil ones, there are a lot of them, they will always do everything in their power to prevent good from succeeding. They want to destroy because they are destruction, and they will survive only so that they can destroy. Their aura is a thick black funnel that leads directly into evil, they are one part of the devil and that is why they all seem the same. They are no longer human. They are in telepathy with Satan. They mock, make foul sounds, lie, create gossip, confuse things, and create pain. They will not even try to explain what they do because they are evil. Warn people about them. There will be a lot of them before the beginning of the end. They are different in a way because they will always be guarding and breathing down on the neck of those they are trying to harm. They will not leave their victims alone. Do not think about them too much because that will only draw them closer to you.

Men are here.

Within each human there is happiness when they are born. When the happiness that is within gets broken, nobody can give it back. That is why everyone is searching for happiness and they try to get it back with different methods. When happiness gets broken, there are things that have happened that cannot be repaired. Bad feelings will be everywhere, replacing all happiness. Like thunder, bad feelings will come, taking away all good feelings and all joy will be gone. Nothing can give back the happiness that has been broken, and nobody can suture those wounds. Only scars remain from one life to the next. Everything will leave behind a bad feeling that cannot be taken away. Then why does this happen? Why do you have to lose happiness, and why do you have to feel bad? Why can't the wounds be healed, and why do people want to hurt each other? When someone is good, everyone wants to hurt them because they are not like others. They are different, you realize that they are like you used to be once a long time ago, and to realize that it hurts. That is why people want to hurt and continue to hurt until the only thing they have left is pain, which will not ease up unless they keep on causing even more pain. Nobody can carry that much pain, and when the pain grows greater, you have to hurt even more so that it can be easier to carry your own pain. This is why there is just too much suffering and pain. Behind all that pain there is always a human whose happiness has been broken.

A-A-A

Men create telepathy.

We come from another star to give this message to our brothers, the Children of Earth. There is a lot of evil here on Earth. There are bodies that can no longer be called human beings, they rape, murder, and do unimaginable things. You will never be able to have your freedom back if you allow this evil to freely continue. From the flying craft comes your friends to help you get that freedom which belongs to you. When you come on Earth, you believe that everyone is good because you are good. As you learn to live here, you have to learn that almost everyone is evil, and you have become much worse yourselves. You cannot stop this process by becoming selfish and evil. The only way you can stop this process is by stopping the evil that is within yourselves. How can you stop it when the evil that you live amongst is everywhere, and if you are good, other people will be evil to you. You must overpower this evil. You must learn how to fight against it. You cannot give up. You must learn how to fight against the evil. When you realize that there is something evil in you, take a large candle and go somewhere to pray so that the evil in you leaves. When you meet evil in other people, do not surrender, but begin a war that will not end until you have conquered it. When Jesus said, "Resist not evil", he meant not to participate in evil, and if someone beats he who is already beaten, they will have bad karma which will not be easy to survive. When Jesus said, "Turn the other cheek...", He meant, do not fight evil with the same methods, but do it right. When you realize that you cannot fight alone and you need help, you must pray for God to send you help. When you receive help, be kind to them so that you may keep them and not send them away.

Men come here.

Children of Earth, the world that you live in has evil everywhere. There is witchcraft, black magic, and all kinds of evil. When you realize that the evil will not go away but will continue to grow, then you will not know what to do anymore. Why don't you begin telepathy with the spirit world which has a lot to say? Telepathy with the spirit world will help you to realize that other planes exist that you are not aware of. There is Heaven and Hell, there are external and internal dimensions that you are unaware of. When you want to be in telepathy with the spirit world, first, you must pray powerfully. You cannot be afraid. When you encounter spirits that want to come and speak with you, you must be ready. When a spirit comes, they will teach and help you to better understand what to do. In a sense, only highly spiritual people are able to do this, the kind that are strong and the kind that receive information about the future. The spirit normally wants to help and guide you so that you may have the strength to handle all evil things on Earth. Provided that you connect with a spirit who lies, then leave them and look for another. You realize that through the spirit world your life can become more fulfilling, like when you are in telepathy with someone who wants to help you and teach you. Like we have explained, you can be in contact with the spirit world. When you pray to God for help, He will send you a protector who wants to help you. You can pray for God to send you a helper who will guide you with the work that you are doing on Earth. Once you receive a spirit, with whom you have an understanding, then you can begin the work that you are doing. You can ask the spirit to further explain things that you do not understand, and you can receive the explanations through a dream, or as visions in your mind, or you can receive the answer in one way or another. The spirit can even whisper things to you that will result in an idea that you would not have on your own. You may even see them.

Every spirit that is good is light in color. If they are dark or black, they are evil and dangerous. This can be a way to learn to live a more spiritual life. Each one of you has your own guide that will follow you everywhere. Telepathy with the spirit world is not always easy because evil spirits always want to come and cause confusion. If you know that you have become possessed, then stop the communication and begin to pray through the body and spirit that you become free from the evil spirits.

Humanoids are not the spirit world. We do not do the kind of work like the spirits who are no longer alive. We produce telepathy directly to Lea's brain and we trust that she knows when the connection is ready. If she begins at the wrong time, she might connect to the spirit world instead. Lying spirits always want to come in between contact with the human and spirit world. They want to disturb and cause harm like they did while they were alive. You should not communicate with them because they are difficult to get rid of. When you want good spirits, you must create light which will allow the spirit to get in contact. If you are depressed or in a bad mental state, the lying or evil spirits can come through your aura body. When you want to have a helper, you can always have a spirit helper. Angels do not do such work, they will only observe you. In a way, they are in between the light and the darkness.

Men come here.

Do not trust anyone, not even in your own selves. The ones on the Path of Four Fires cannot even trust themselves. When you came on Earth, you had nothing, and when you leave, you will leave with a lot. You will know the crazy, the beautiful, the poor, and the rich. You will meet a lot of people, but only a few will stay for the rest of your lives. Why can't you keep all the people that you know near you? This is because each one of you has a different soul, and when you meet someone whose reincarnations, mind, and spirit is too different, you will not have much you can share with each other. When you meet someone who has similar thoughts and whose life is different, you will not have much in common. When you meet someone who has a similar soul, then you will spend a lot of time together because you want the same things, but when you meet with one that has the same kind of soul, then you will always be together, because of the way you were made. When you meet someone who has had similar experiences you can talk a lot together. When you meet someone who is an old soul like you are, then you will enjoy each other's company. When you meet someone who is as intelligent as you are, you can be comfortable. When you meet those that were from your past Path of the Four Fires reincarnations, you will want to spend a lot of time together. When you meet someone from another country, you want them to get to know you and spend time with you so that you do not have to be so alone.

When humans grow up, they no longer know how to talk and share thoughts as children do. Adults want to withdraw into loneliness, and they want to be alone and not disturbed. When children are alone, they want to meet with a lot of other children to talk and examine. Many think that foreigners are different. They think that they can understand them better, but everyone is different from each other and if you are not understood in our own country, you will not be better understood anywhere else either. When humans have been on Earth for long enough, they will want someone to help them learn how to love, and they want to be loved. This is a very important lesson, and many are born to learn about love. When you try and try and you are not loved, maybe you can learn something from that. When you learn to live alone, you will learn to love yourselves. That is why it is also important to learn how to live alone, so that you know who you are and what you want, so that no one else can do harm to you, unless you allow it to happen. When you do not know who is what kind of human, you just have to get to know them by meeting and talking. You will know how to differentiate good and evil humans from each other.

Men are here.

Here up in Heaven, we do not have the same kinds of problems as you do down on Earth. We do not rape children or animals, and we do not do wrong things to each other. Life here is peaceful and happy. We do not even know how to be jealous of each other. We can trust that nobody will hurt anyone else, and nobody will want to talk bad about one another. Humans cannot live like this. Although we trust each other, we do not want someone to take away those things that we already have. Why do humans do that all the time, where they want to take away something that someone else already has? Why do people do such things? When you meet someone who wants to take away your life and everything that you have, why do they want to do that? They cannot live your life, nobody can live anyone else's life. Everyone has to live their own life, and there is no other option. Nobody can take someone else's life, no matter how much they try. It is not possible, no matter how much someone can try to copy another.

By helping you serve God, by sacrificing you help yourselves with your own karma, and by teaching you will receive a part of that infinite information that will never end. If you want to love, then love the life that is everywhere. Love animals, children, and those who do not have love. The promise of Heaven is such that you can love and be happy without receiving love. With sacrifice you can overcome bad karma. Although, even if you sacrificed your whole life, not all karma will be gone. There are many different sacrifices.

When you sacrifice for love, you will receive light.

When you sacrifice your pride, you will receive a lot of harmony.

When you sacrifice your hate, you will receive a lot of love.

When you sacrifice your life, you can overcome difficult illnesses.

If you want, you can always choose your own destiny. Sometimes you do not care, you just say, "It doesn't matter, I was evil, and I will take what I am even if I cannot handle it all.", and when you get everything, you can pay with your new life. If you do not have the strength, you will become angry, envious, and evil. Who are those who do not know that they have helped a lot? What kind are those who do not know they are evil? What kind are those seasons that never change? When someone has helped a lot and they do not know that they have lived by helping others, they are the ones who have come to help. When someone has helped and then taken from everything, they have changed to an evil spirit. Sometimes, an evil spirit will choose a new life by taking someone's body and sending away the spirit that lived in it. When the evil spirit that comes wants someone's body, the spirit needs to be helped to become free. There are many who have evil spirits, not everything can be explained with psychology. When you think that someone is controlled by an evil spirit, you just have to pray so that the evil spirit leaves its victim. Do not ever trust psychics. They are always more or less under the control of the spirit world. Many have trusted them to be able to fulfill their dreams and then have been misled.

Everyone has their own through the body and the spirit, but not everyone can meet if they have bad karma. Sometimes, soulmates are in different levels of spiritual development. If you can meet your soulmate, begin by being completely quiet and see what happens. The Earth takes its own and the spirit takes its own. The spirit will always go with their soulmate whether they want to or not. The body wants to help and follow the spirit. When you meet your soul mate, you will realize that you cannot be separated from each other even if you wanted to. Sometimes, soulmates are friends that cannot be separated, but they are always a man and a woman, never two men or two women. Even though you want to have your own, sometimes it is not for the best. Nobody can learn unless they live with different kinds of people. Love and understanding can develop between different people, but it will never be like it is in spiritual couples.

We have a lot of telepathy here in our flying saucer from the other world that you do not know. In the other world, there are many who have lived on Earth and were finally able to get out. Beings similar to humans have always been among you through body and spirit. You just do not know them. They help the ones who have telepathy from the flying saucers, which means that those who are in telepathy with the ones in the flying saucer are usually Men's own.

Some of you have unreasonable difficulties because humans are evil, and they do not even recognize their own evilness. Some have to pay the price for what others do without any sense of responsibility. Provided that you cannot get away from this kind of life situation, then it is better to leave and go away.

Provided that you want to know, we can explain why it is so difficult on Earth. You come here as you were new, but what happens? You come to a new body and when you begin life, you realize that everything that you lived through has already happened before. You will realize that there is nothing new, and that everything is good and evil. In this way, you will have the opportunity to reconcile and correct everything in a new way. Unfortunately, you just do not learn. You make the same mistakes again and again. Nothing will help you in your future life because your new life is always a little worse. However, you are still given another opportunity to try again. In your last life you will have to go through hell to overcome all the bad karma that you still have not learned. Provided that in your last life you do not learn, then you will not have another chance to try, you will go into damnation. Which means that you will disintegrate and stop existing. Provided that you do not live in another plane, where resides primitive demons who lack all sense, are without a soul, and who are Satan's slaves. These creatures are half low creatures and half alive. They will remain in the other plane and they are no longer allowed to be a part of spiritual development. They can feel like others, but their feelings are almost completely gone. They just exist, and in this way, they pay for breaking God's Laws too many times.

When a demon like this comes to temp you, maybe in another life you may have been dependent on them. Maybe you served them and did favors for them when they were in purgatory with a lot of karma. You depended on them. This is why you should never start a relationship for solely physical reasons. This beautiful person might be a demon who will take you with them to Hell. You must be strong so that you can survive life. Not just any choice is the right one. You have to know what you do. There are no excuses for choices that were wrong. If you have made a wrong choice, you will have to pay a high price for it. Provided that you do not want to pay that price, then you will have to redeem it with your own life. Because of this, life is serious and difficult. Even if you were confused, you are responsible for all of your actions to God.

Provided that you would like to know what you should do, so that you do what is right, you will know if you are causing suffering to yourselves or to another human being. If you cause pain to another then you have made wrong choices. You have to know what causes suffering to others. You cannot say, "I didn't know that this caused him pain." You know who suffered from what. There is no escape with which you can defend yourself. After the choices have been made it is too late to regret. Everything that you have done you are responsible for. You can still start everything again from the beginning as long as you are still alive, and in this way, you can redeem your wrong choices if you want to, but there is nothing that can undo what has already been done. Provided that you want to know what you can do to change your lives, we say that you can look at your actions directly in the eye and be honest. Look at what you have wanted and why. When you realize what you really want, then you have really understood something. Provided that you have a serious psychological disorder, it may be that you have it so that you would do things that otherwise, you would not want to do, and once again this is karma. Helping fulfill the payment of karma.

Provided that you can ever survive all of this, then you will be given the other world that we have previously mentioned. This world and the other world, they have nothing in common, so do your best so that you can one day detach from the karma and bonds of the Children of the Earth. Provided that you want to help yourselves, you can find the right meditation, but nothing, no sacrifice, no meditation, nothing will free you from the responsibility that you have from the choices you have made. There is nothing that will free you from bad karma except atonement, and there is nothing that will set you free from your responsibilities and your choices. When one day you are strong enough so that you will no longer want to make wrong choices, then you have defeated karma. This will mean that you have entered the other world that we have not even begun to explain. How can you even imagine that you would be ready for this other world if you have not yet learned anything here.

Men come back. We will start from the beginning.

Children of the Earth, we do not think like you do, you will realize that. We are not like you. You want things which are useless to you. You want everything without realizing that everything that you want also has its consequences. When you want yourself to have everything that everyone else has, you are only part of the mind. You will become a part of the matter that this world is made of. When you overcome your desire to want things, you can also develop spiritually. When you overcome this desire and you live like you did when you came into this life, then you can still build wealth with your body, but you will no longer be stuck in this matter in spirit. When you are no longer held by matter in spirit, then you can become free. You can produce your spiritual and material life, but you will not become a ghost and stay haunting after your death but instead you can leave your material life behind. You will realize the difference between the spiritual and material life, and you will not be imprisoned by matter.

When you are alive, you are no longer only a spirit, and when you die, you will only be a spirit. During your life, you have to learn how to separate the spirit and the body. Provided that you do not learn, there is nothing you can do about it when you die. After you have died you can no longer say that the body was born to die and the spirit to remain. After death, you cannot do anything about it, life has passed you and everything that you have done has already been done. You cannot live your lives and say, "I didn't know what life was about."

The Storks are here.

The body was a part of evolution and was allowed to come into life, like nature and all animals. It was embodied through evolution; it traveled a difficult history of development until it became as it is. God created man in His own image. Humanoids are in God's image; our bodies are much more translucent in matter compared to yours. Our bodies are not as yours are. We can travel in your thought world. We can travel like any ghost, but unlike them we are not dead. Men who you love and whom you would want to return to are such matter. The low self does not affect their body.

When God created outer space, He allowed the world to become such that it would be perfect. When He allowed the world to become perfect, He allowed Satan to come to the world. As you will come to understand, the world cannot be perfected without Satan. When Satan came, he wanted to be as God is, he became the opposite of God. He created the underworld, the low spirit, and the body, and both the high spirit and the low spirit stepped in. They had to be the center of this power struggle. God allowed the world to develop in its own way.

He allowed the fires to come,

He allowed the Earth to come,

and He allowed the water to come. He allowed everything to be settled in its own place. Everything developed at its own pace so that there was harmony in all development, and when harmony came, came the body of the human who developed under its own laws. When the body was developed the spirit could settle down to live in it. Both the spirit created by God, and the one created by Satan.

When God said to Eve, "In pain you shall bring children", He means that without pain the body cannot give birth. When the times were much higher spiritually, it could. As the new image of thought during the times of higher spirituality the spirit body could. Nowadays, the humanoids give birth like humans but without pain. We do not feel pain like you because our bodies are more translucent, and our bodies are not subject to such laws as yours. Although we do die, our bodies become thinner and just wither away. We will remain in our other spirit matter. Ghosts are not such matter as we are. They are spirit matter like the spirit, but unlike Men they are dead.

Humanoids will come to live among you like regular humans. We will come among you alive in human bodies. The body that Men carry can be forced to be like your body. We can create a state where we become flesh without being born as a human.

As your thought world nowadays is very narrow, and your choices are wrong, you will understand spiritual matters less and less. It is difficult for you to accept spiritual thoughts because you are no longer spiritually awake. When you pray, and you cannot find a connection to God, you might be in telepathy with Satan, and you cannot break this bond. When you realize that your entire life has been in telepathy with Satan, you might be in big trouble.

When you go back to your early childhood, you will realize that the body you had then did not follow you to adulthood. You will come to telepathy which you had as a child. You wanted for everything that belongs to you to be the body, that you will live forever, and that you will always love. This is how you were. You did not think of Satan, and you did not want to hurt another. When you grew older you changed because you began making choices at a very early age. When today you are adults, and you want to be worthy of your past promises, you no longer know what you are.

When you want to become good, and you want to love, you no longer know how to love, and as you approach death you are like bleached flour sacks from which all the flour has been put away, and even the shell no longer has any color. You can no longer fulfill this emptiness no matter how much you try because the time that you had has passed. When you die, you will disintegrate like a fire that burns in Hell. If there was anything in you through the low self, you will become a slave of the low self. Even if you were not evil, you will be burned in fire. The Ones brought by the earth, fire, and air are the Children of the Earth. Read from the Bible stories about Hell, where dry branches are burning. The body will be buried on Earth. The body does not burn in Hell, but the spirit without development will burn like branches that no one wants.

Men are here.

Children of the Earth, you will come to a time when there are no more decent people like Men, who are at the top of the heavens and whom you are not allowed to meet. When this time comes, tomorrow will no longer come. Provided that you still wish for others to reveal the truth, you are badly mistaken. There will no longer be bodies who can come and reveal this truth. As you will learn to know, this body who will reveal the truth (Lea) has been Men's own since she was a small child. We are not claiming that she did not have many weaknesses. She continued to burn in fire. This fire was from Satan who did not want to leave her. Because of this, she had to do many things to be able to continue this work. She will do what she can. We are not claiming that she was pure like the angels in Heaven, there were others who were purer than her, but she will defeat Satan, and that is the greatest achievement anyone can do during life. The spirit who has defeated Satan is a Great Spirit, whom everyone who has died and everyone who is alive will respect.

When you do not know who Satan is, you cannot defeat him. You are perhaps a part of Satan's large body that he wants to create on Earth. He wants to practice so much magic here that all who are from God will have to go, and once they have left, there will be no more hope. When this time comes you will know. You can no longer find anything good, not even from pure children. Even the children will be evil. Only evil spirits will come to Earth. The dogs will go mad, no one can no longer have a dog as a pet. The dogs will begin killing humans whom they hate. Dogs are good animals; Men take care of all that God has created.

In accordance to a Law that God created, the Storks are such who can bring clarity to life. The Storks will create a new past life. We will begin a cleansing on this planet. We will cleanse this when it will all be over. We will begin by returning the men and we will help them to find their women. We will begin this purification when all of Satan's own are gone, when the planet is completely destroyed and there is nothing left. Only those who gather your history for the sake of the future, after all else is gone, they have your stories, some of your lives and some of your people. They take bodies that are used by their own, you could not live in their vibrational level. They will take bodies in which the spirit of one of their own lives. Through these bodies they will reproduce new humans so everything can begin again. When everything starts from the beginning, we will come back again after you had to leave. We will start new history where all the secrets of what had happened before are hidden. We will create a new culture for you and build you a new beginning which you will begin to destroy again after you take Satan back into your lives. You can no longer get rid of him. Although many are able to come back to continue everything from the beginning, their history will be difficult, and finally, provided that they defeat Satan, they will have passed what we call, the Men's Path of The Four Fires.

At the times of the end there are still spirits here whose purpose is to maintain God's light. They are martyrs who volunteer to come back from God's Kingdom only for the sake of the little ones and those who cannot prevent their destiny. Those are the ones who want salvation in a very short time. They will soon be murdered like everyone who has God's light, they will be killed in body, but their spirit will remain living. When suddenly during their dreams they realize all the signs they are receiving, they will just want to come back to God. They are the last reborn coming back to the Earth. They are the last who will be the first to receive the new beginning. They are the kinds of spirits who had served Satan without realizing who their master was. They thought they had served God, but during the end times their soul's closed eyes opened, and they will want to embody their own spirit to be able to sacrifice it for God. They will die a martyr's death, and they will be persecuted. They will search for all our own who are still on Earth. They search for them regardless of what will happen to them.

Men will leave some of our own here to help people. Our own can be at peace from Satan because he cannot do anything to them. They will support those who are falling and help the ones who sacrifice themselves to God. These who repented at the last moment will be searching for them (Men's own) so that they can receive the light. They look for them like crazy. Like those whose only salvation is a small straw of hay. They know who are our own. During these times nobody will doubt them. They can live together during this last mission on Earth, and they are helpers whom no one dares to harm.

Finally, there are those born again who have defeated Satan in their previous life and they have become powerful. Satan can no longer touch them. They only want to help with their body and spirit. Those who overcame their bodies will talk about God's Kingdom. Those are the martyrs. Those who Satan did not tempt in spirit, but in body, which they have to give as a sacrifice for their defeat. They will return to help again and again, to sacrifice their body for the sake of God.

As you can realize, you will never be left alone. Although you have chosen Satan and you want to repent, if you want to repent you will be given a helper, usually someone we have sent. When you are given help, you can begin the battle which will never be easy. When the battle is finished, you can begin a meditation through which you can strengthen the spirit that is weak. When the spirit is weak, you will really need to support all the time. Many mornings when you wake up and you feel that everything in your life was for nothing, you will realize that your spirit has not grown, and this you mourn. Not what you have done while working.

You just do not understand your own sadness that is spiritual, not material, and when you realize that your spirit is weak you need strengthening. When you need strengthening it is better that you spend time alone, that you pray a lot, do the spiritual cleansing, and that you withdraw to solitude where you can learn to listen to the differences of the human body, mind, and spirit.

When you do not come to Earth to seek the truth, then what do you seek? When you do not search for the truth, you search for daydreams, changes and lies. And when you are searching for the dreams that you want to live, you are searching for Satan who will fulfill your dream. When you live searching for the truth, the truth is not what you want. Maybe the body is only a small, beautiful home where you live for a moment, and when your time is full you will leave it, like you will leave everything else that you have.

When you want to be loved, you dress the body beautiful, and you do what you can so that everyone will want your body. However, the body can only love another body under the laws of the Earth. The body can fall in love with another body, but only for a short time. Once it gets to know this body, it will find another. This is why many spirit beings choose to live in such a body that is not funny, and does not produce any other desires, because they are searching for someone who loves their spirit. When they give up their physical beauty, they come back to search for a spirit who loves them as a spiritual being. These types of spirits have often violated against love and want atonement. They usually do not find love because they have not deserved it. Love must always be earned. When love escapes you like a shadow, you do not deserve it. You have to learn to love right. The only true love is spiritual love because the love between spirits is eternal. When two spirits love each other, nobody can prevent them. Although they would not meet during life, they meet in the spirit world. When they meet in life, they do not care about people's rules or talks. They live with the body they have, and they will become happy despite all obstacles. The love of the spirit is not like the love of the body, it differs from the love of the body in many different ways. When the spirit loves, it will know from the time that it is a baby that the one it loves will always be near. The spirit feels the love that is near it all the time. The closer this person comes the stronger the feeling of love grows.

Usually, the spirit knows that it can soon meet the one it loves, and the spirit is alert and searching all the time. Many have even ended their previous relationships without any apparent reason.

The spirit waits, not knowing through the body. The body does not want to know what the spirit knows. The body is subject to the Earth's laws, and it can go crazy from all the information that is transmitting from the spirit. For this reason, you have to grow in spirit to be able to live in the world of the spirit. The body's love is only subject to the laws of the Earth. As per the laws of the Earth it is to give birth and produce new bodies. These bodies want to reproduce together, and as per the laws of the Earth they want to find many bodies whom they can love. If the body only wants to keep one body to love then that body is very similar to it.

Like the spirit who is searching for its pair, (soulmate) the body is also searching for a partner. It keeps another body that is like it is as its own pair. That is why many when searching for a spouse choose someone who looks similar. When the time on Earth is finished under the laws of the body, there will be nothing left of the love. When the spouses die, they are no longer together, nor want to meet again. This type of a relationship can sometimes be a lesson if the other one is a very different type of spirit, and this would be the only way to bring them together. When the lesson is learned there will be nothing left of the love, other than what it never was.

When spirit couples die, they will become even closer to each other. This does not mean that they would be a couple of two men or two women who want to live together. They are always a man and a woman. God does not do such a thing that the one who loves the other as a man and a woman would be the same sex. Even if they would be, they would not want to think of anything sexual. All sexual relationships between the same sex are from Satan. The only meaning of that is to ridicule God's holy purpose. Under God's Laws, nobody can love someone of the same sex. When Satan is searching for victims, he will give them many horrific things that through their body they can fulfill. When Satan wants a certain spirit to become contaminated with love for the same sex, he fills this body with filthy spirits of the opposite sex which make this body desire the same sex. Many have horrendous incestual experiences which through their body they do not want to remember, and they will seek same sex sexual relationships for this reason. However, this is only sexual love, and they do not even want to search for spiritual love.

When the human becomes aware that he is a spirit, he is no longer bonded to earthly actions.

Although he will hate the representative of the other sex, he does not hate all of them. He knows that the one who wounded and hurt him was a low-level spirit and he realizes that each human is different.

When you are no longer like God created you, then you are more and more in the low self's spirit, the image like Satan has created of himself. All bodies one day have to die, your spirit is what you were through your bodies. When you no longer care what will happen, then you are Satan's own. The body is just the body. It is neither good nor bad, it is just subjected to its own laws. When the body takes over, you will do what it wants, and you will face many problems when you die. When you allow the low self to guide your life, when you die you will become a part of Satan's spirit, and through his spirit you will produce evil telepathy to people who do not know you. In this face nobody will know you, you will lose your own identity. But when you live in spirit, and you have a strong spirit, you will enter another level where you can continue to develop yourselves. You can find all those who you have loved in spirit. When you come back you will be even more spiritual than what you were in your past life. When the time comes where Satan himself comes to Earth, you will no longer be here. Everyone with spiritual development will be taken away.

When Satan is on Earth, all his own will become flesh and can do whatever they want. When Satan destroys this planet, nobody here will want to know why the ones burning in fire are those whom Satan loves. When currently he is only a spirit, he will live like he once was alive. When he comes, there is no one who can be saved anymore. He will only come to get his own. These are the kind who no longer have any other telepathy but Satan's.

Everyone will want him to be the leader of the world because he will begin his speech about peace.

"We will become a part of history and we will leave in peace, and when we leave, we will bring peace with us."

When he speaks, the spell begins. Everyone will bother others when they speak, but when he speaks, everyone will be silent. When he comes, even the crazy will be quiet.

When he hypnotizes people, with the help of his body he will produce a lot of comfortable joy. People will admire his pleasant appearance and when he holds his hand over someone's head, they will become gentle and loving. When this change happens, people will begin to believe he is God sent. The body is only receiving hypnosis that Satan gives, and the body will change because of the effect of the hypnosis. The body cannot prevent this because it is under the laws of the Earth, and when the spirit does not agree with the body, it will create painful mental and spiritual states. Through the body, this body is only receiving the hypnosis that Satan gives and the body only changes due to the hypnosis in accordance to the laws of the Earth and the body cannot prevent this, and when the spirit is not in an agreement with the body the painful agonizing mental/spiritual states will begin.

Like we have previously explained, Satan will come as good, not as evil. He comes like the devil comes as a snake who no one recognizes, not even his own. When he leaves, he will leave like he came, no one will know where he disappeared to. He just wants to take power over his own. He will destroy the entire planet Earth and with him he will bring evil spirits who will take care of the hell that follows. When humans finally realize that he is Satan himself, it will all be too late, no one can be saved, this will be the worst. The helpers will still be here, they will be here the entire time like we have promised with the help of the body. (physically) They are on a much worse level than others. They know that Satan himself has arrived, and their spirit has to suffer all the time from the vibrations that are destructive. They are here only to witness what will happen, they will write everything down and they will make physical sacrifices. They draw the filth towards themselves to be able to clean it. This is a burdensome mission that some of our own will do. They no longer help anyone; they will only try to clean the vibrations so that the animals and the bodies that are just bodies can tolerate it before their death without further suffering.

The animals will go mad. They will no longer swallow what they should, they refuse to eat, and they hate the human beings who are now completely evil. Even cats will be skin and bone. They would rather not eat than eat anything that has been blessed by Satan. The world that once was a beautiful place will evaporate like the rain in the air. Everyone who was born in a new way will die through the body and spirit of Satan. This death is, in a sense, the last of the reincarnations. If someone among them wants to amend what they have done, they will no longer have a chance. Satan's time on Earth is brief. An attempt will be made to execute him because he speaks of peace, but war is near. When the attempt to execute him is made, he will become even more powerful because it is a satanic scheme. When one of his own wants to kill him, he will become even more powerful. This evil is worse than evil. That is why he wants it to happen. If one of our own kills him, he will die, but as we have explained, none of our own wants to kill him. They want that he, like his brothers take with him those who belong to him.

When it is all over, we will return here to build everything again. When history begins from the beginning, the new time will come, and when the new time has come, the others will come, who have been waiting so that they can come. When judgment has passed and everything is over, there will be no more evil here. We will come back and build the history of the Earth again from the beginning. When you know what the stories of karma used to be, you will really know that mythology is a story from the previous era, before the coming of the Children of the Earth. You cannot understand these stories which are very symbolic because you cannot receive the information as it is today.

When you do not think about anything, you also are nothing. Without thoughts, you are like an animal whose spirit has been destroyed, an empty body that lives under the laws of the Earth. You cannot live when the spirit has completely fallen asleep. When the spirit is asleep, you are only half alive and you waste your entire life, which could be your last.

Men are here.

When you want life to be beautiful and good, then do not leave God. Humanoids live near the stars and near God. Men's living life here is fun and beautiful. God never said that life cannot be fun. You can be happy, have little gatherings and live a regular life. Nobody becomes evil from happy things, just the opposite. Humans and everything that has been created needs happy things so that life can be physical and comfortable enough. When you want to develop spiritually, you can still live like you want. You can go out and spend time with your family and meet new people. This will not prevent a spiritual life. You can still read books and when you want you can watch movies like you used to. Nothing like that is an obstacle for spiritual development. We are not saying that you cannot live a regular life when you want someone to love you. That does not prevent your spiritual development. There are however some laws that in your pleasures you have to follow. One is that you cannot only live for things that give you pleasure.

When it is time that the others come, you might not be ready. When you are not ready, you will not know when they are here. The others are the kind who will come to take their own, they can come at anytime. This mainly means contact. We search for contact with those who are ready. When we come and you are not ready, we will leave and we will not come back. When you do not care who it is that comes and takes you, then you are still Satan's own. Everyone who understands things knows to be afraid of Satan. Those who do not take care of their only spirit have left it to Satan. When we come to take our own, we come like a thief. You will never know when we were there and when we leave. We will come like we began this writing, nobody knew the moment, not even us. As you know, now Men will come to take their own. When we find one of our own, we will begin contact. This contact can exist on any level. We can only be in contact for a short while, but when the contact has been established it will remain for the rest of their life. Many will come and meet us during dreams. We come to your dreams and we will explain things that you will also remember when you come back to your body. These types of contacts we have many. Many believe that they are the only ones and they are too afraid to talk about this. It is different if you are in contact with others or with the evil ones. Then you will be gone like the wind. This means that the evil ones can produce a type of connection that you cannot stop, and makes life an ongoing funeral, so do not be too naïve, not all messages are from Men.

Men produce happiness and you will receive the effect from the spirit which becomes stronger. When the evil ones come, you will start slowly losing your mind and no one will be able to help you. When you go crazy, life becomes meaningless and in the end, you just want to die. When you die, you will get rid of them, provided that you are not evil. However, the body does not want to live if the evil energies make it feel sick.

When we come we always have a message. We never come without explaining something and after this your conciseness expands. When you meet us, do not be afraid. Humanoids that are good will never cause you any harm. The ones you find evil or strange are not Men. All of those who are our own will meet us during sleep. We will look for them, so be awake when we come. When we say awake, we mean that you must be spiritually awake. If you are not spiritually awake your spirit will cry and complain," Please set me free." This is the cry that the spirit cries to the body for help, "Body set me free." When the body is in control and you cannot prevent its desires, then you cannot live as you should.

You imagine that you are a part of such origin that you are a part of Men, however this belief is not enough. Even if you prove it to others with your own connection, this is not enough for us. Men do not care what people think. When Men look you in the eye and we can see your pathetic spirit, it is not enough that you believe in what you believe in. The truth is the truth no matter what, with the laws of the body it can never fulfill the truth. Provided that you would live like one of Men, you do not know how we live. The angels know, and God knows. The low self can never be a part of the lives of God's Children. If you still live in a sinful way, you can never be one of us. This means that you cannot live under any law that you do not know.

When you meet our own you do not know them. You think that they are strange, angels, or different from you. They are not like Earth's evil children. You realize that they have a strange secret life, which does not mean that they would be slaves to drugs or alcohol. Although, in some level, some are behind in their spiritual development. Those who cannot be strong anymore have fallen. When our own fall, it is dangerous for themselves and others. They can become incredibly evil. Those who we call crazy are ones who in their own small dark world think that they are spiritually developed but are not. This world is red because it is close to Hell.

They think that they are good and funny and rather spiritually developed but they only pretend to be as such. Their narrow-minded world that lacks warmth and love is easy to reveal, they are only pretenders. Their only mission is to prove to others how good they are, instead of even trying to be good. Beware of them, they will always explain what good people they are, although a lifetime has passed with no proof of that goodness. Once they penetrate into your lives, beware, they always have some scheme created by Satan in their minds. They do not even realize what they are doing. They always say afterwards that they did not mean any harm. When they do not leave you alone, you will get to know them and no matter what you do, you cannot get rid of them. The only way to get rid of them is to remain in the truth. Finally, they will not be able to handle the speeches you give them, and they will leave. When you trust someone like that you will never know whom they will owe your life to, and when you cannot trust them, get rid of them.

The body is what it is, it ages prematurely. It is only subject to the laws of the Earth. When the spirit ages, it does not seem older. When the spirit gets old and its time comes, it will only appreciate more spiritual things. When the spirit is young, it does not want to think spiritual things, it always chooses what it wants. When the spirit is old, it no longer wants to disturb life that does not belong to it. It chooses a way of life that is better suited for its nature. It wants you to practice meditation, to be able to be near it, and it wants you to make the right choices. When the spirit is evil, it does not want new changes, all spiritual things bother it. When the spirit is old and evil, it is also dangerous. If it wants spiritual things, it only wants them from Satan, and once it learns Satan's teachings it becomes worse.

When a certain low spirit wanted to have a new home once more, the reason it happened was because they had to seduce a man. The low spirit had to seduce a man who had made terrible mistake because of love. From the beginning it was able to cast the necessary spells. This low spirit caused a lot of suffering during its life. It had to be born on Earth because of her brother. The low spirit's brother was here and he had to create a lot of suffering to everyone who was near him. When that was achieved, it went away and joined Satan. This story is here to explain that sometimes an evil spirit will become flesh only for a specific purpose. This brother who was the low sprit's brother wanted to become like the other sister's low spirit was. For this reason, the sister also came to help him. They became evil and they wanted everyone who knew them to also become a part of Satan. They knew a lot of people and the man who was seduced in the end stabbed himself in the stomach with a knife to be able to have peace.

The reason for this story was that the Storks do not always come and explain what the truth is. When you want to hear the truth, you have to learn how to find it on your own. The man who had died now had regrets and wanted reform. When he came back on Earth, he began by being completely alone so that he could learn what love is. He never complained that he was alone, for him it was very natural. This story of the low spirit is true, Men do not want to reveal who he is. When the low spirit left, it left without ever returning.

When you do not want to know who is who, how can your brother know you? You think that anybody can be right to you. Anyone's body can be right, the body is always satisfied, and it can choose any body for it to feel good. The spirit cannot be satisfied with just anything. If it can, it will only choose those who are right for it. When you make a wrong choice against your spirit, you will have to live with the truth that you have made a crime against your spirit, and when you have made a crime against your spirit, there is price you have to pay. The worst price is that you can never be happy, regardless of the good that happens. You will always have a bad feeling. When you do not think of what the price of your choices are, whatever you choose to do, it will always be under the laws of karma. When you live to be old, you will think of what kind of life you lived. You will live in pain that you cannot take away. As a result, the body will produce incurable illnesses, and you want to forget your entire life. When your choices were correct, you can enjoy life, love, and the memories of love, even when you are older.

Men begin.

Children of the Earth, time that you waste in all things that are fun and you remail in a state where you do not care about the laws of the body or the laws of the spirit, it becomes a threat to your spirit that cannot wait forever for you to begin to be in contact with it. When you waste your time in everything that does not develop you, you are wasting your only life. When you have wasted your life, you might not find it again when you come back to Earth and start everything again. You might not find what you need to find. When you are not in contact with your spirit then you are in contact with your low spirit, or your own mind, and when you receive telepathy from the low spirit you might not find your spirit anymore, the spirit that you had in the beginning. The body wants power, the low self wants power, and when you give that power then you can no longer find the spirit that God gave you. When you want to find your spirit, you have to find a meditation that will help you to find your spirit. If you cannot find a meditation you can still pray with the new method, we taught. When you pray you should always begin the same way with, "Our Father" When you begin, your telepathy might go to the low spirit and to Satan. You have to be very careful for that reason. When you begin your prayer, it is best that you start with, "In the name of Jesus Christ Our Father's and Heavens Kingdoms." And after that continue with, "Our Father." This, "Who are in Heaven," can also be Satan who is also in heaven. (Heaven in reference to space) He is a bodiless spirit who is also in space like God is. When Jesus gave this prayer, he originally explained that it should begin with the name of His body, He is the one who is in between God and the Children of the Earth. He is the one who unites life and spirit, and through Him, you will begin your prayer.

We just want to give this as a reminder that Jesus was one of us. He was one of us, He was just the purest and closest to God than any other, and in that was the only Son of God. When you do not know the person who comes and asks you to go with them, then do not go. You will meet many who will say that they are from Jesus Christ and will want you to follow. When you start searching for Jesus from the Earth, because He promised to come back, He will never come and say, "I am Jesus Christ", read the new coming of Christ again from the Bible. Jesus will come as the light that has been absent for a long time. Humanoids will only produce the coming of Christ. He will come to bring the light and when Satan comes, Jesus will influence this because when Jesus comes on Earth Satan will be gone. Satan does not want to be here any longer when Jesus comes. He (Satan) will leave with his herd, which many have already died and many more will continue to die. When Jesus comes, there will not be many humans left, some will have died of disease, some will have died in the fires of the Earth, and some will have died in the nature body's vibrations. (Earthquakes)

When there are only a few people left, Jesus will come. He comes to bring the light that before Him did not exist. He will bring the light that will remain here for a thousand years. After a thousand years have passed, Satan will come back with his angels. They will be born here again to destroy what Jesus has created. They will start evil again. There are bodies that can no longer be purified everywhere, when Satan comes. This means that everyone who is here then will be contaminated. They will choose a time when all good is gone and Men want that through dreams and visions from telepathy, we will witness all this. As time reaches its end, many will receive gifts that they did not have before. This will be the final warning. Satan will only come to get his own. When you think that you are Satan's own when you get sick, don't be sad. When you have to live through this time, where many will die of incurable diseases, do not be afraid. This is just a way of how Satan will come to take his own away. Many whom do not belong to Satan also have to get sick, only so that they can return sooner. Only the ones who are Satan's own will be gone from here for good. When in this way the Earth is purified, there will come a time where Jesus comes back. He will only come to get his own, like Satan came to get his own. Because Jesus will come back, the Earth has to be purified. The spirit that resides in a body that cannot be destroyed has to come to a man that is pure. This man who will be Jesus will be as pure as God Himself. His coming is such that you will not even know what has happened. Suddenly, He will be among you, and He will choose men and women who will always remain near him. When He leaves, He will choose the best of them to go with Him, and Men will come to pick Him up. He will no longer die on Earth. He will come to Men and stay with us, He will also teach us here.

After this has happened, you will realize that all those bodies that are here on Earth are the kind that are pure, no one is contaminated, and nobody wants to contaminate themselves. Although you will come to live during a time that has never been here on Earth before, you should know that Satan is still waiting so that he can come back. For this reason, everyone who is aware of what will happen will also be held responsible. For the one who knows is responsible for that knowledge, the ones who do not know as much cannot be responsible for everything. Who is the one who comes first? And who is the one who leaves last? What we have explained, we have explained that regardless of bad thoughts you can relax. Although you think everything is hopeless, that the time for the light is over, and that Men are gone, the time that is best is still ahead. When you reach a time in which you have passed, you will realize that that was a bad time, where you had no knowledge nor light. This time that will come will be the first that will have as much light that it will have.

Humanoids that you continue to meet are evil. They are from Satan's lower space craft. They want to be seen so that you think all humanoids are evil. They cause a lot of pain, and they use evil telepathy on all of their victims. They have masks that make them look like Others, who are not evil. In reality, the evil ones do not look like they seem to look. They want to prevent the work that the Others are doing on Earth. They destroy the mark that the Others leave on Earth and choose as their victims those who are the key people to the Others. These Others that we have spoken about are different than Men. They look like small creatures who are spiritually unkind. They are not quite like Men are, but they are not evil. They have work on Earth. They want humans to be kind to animals and to stop destroying the Earth. They preserve animals and abduct humans to their crafts to observe their vibrations. They might create a red paralysis state that you cannot explain. This red paralysis state is the kind that you become red and cannot breathe. This is caused by vibrations that are too different compared to humans. The evil humanoids do not cause this. They produce severe pain resembling mental states that you have to live with. You can no longer be among other people and you will isolate yourselves completely and think of yourselves as the loneliest people on Earth. This evil energy that they produce is the kind that you will always want to die. The Others are in big trouble with these evil ones, the Others do not want to harm the human's spirit, or the human. The evil ones only want to harm and the telepathy they produce can make a human go crazy. Many will become paranoid. They will feel like they are being persecuted and many can only defend themselves by praying in the light.

Beware of the evil humanoids, they are difficult to get rid of. When they have taken a victim, when you think that something like that has happened, begin the cleansing method we have previously mentioned. If even that does not help, leave for a short while and continue the cleansing. Sometimes, they cannot find the victim immediately, and when you are able to get your vibrational level higher they can no longer do anything. Provided that you are in contact with the Others, you will become otherwise restless and can have trouble sleeping, and you want to speak about humanoids and you do not want to be alone. You feel helpless because of this connection and you feel that you are connected to something but do not know what this something is. This connection can cause severe states of fear. Although they are not evil, their magnetic field is just so different that when it enters a human's spirit field it causes a state that nowadays is called a magnetic state of fear. This fear is not ordinary fear. As you know they are different kinds of humanoids both with their physical and spiritual structure. However, they still want to remain close to a human being to be able to refine a being who is cross bred between them and a human. This being will unite them with humans. We are not in direct contact with them although in a certain sense we are. They are too different from Men.

The evil ones produce severe states of pain and spiritual disturbance, mental disorders and isolation, shakiness, headaches, and sexual conditions. You might experience a tremor that you cannot understand. You might feel tremors which are caused by their telepathy. Your entire spirit begins to tremble, you become sensitive to crying, and you start to forget things. You might sleep talk in a way that might scare someone. When you sink into boredom, you cannot think, you can no longer concentrate on anything, and or you cannot stay still. Instead, you will run in circles like you are escaping something, and at times you do not even know who you are anymore. Then most likely you are in contact with the evil humanoid's spirit world. The Others can cause restlessness and states of fear, called magnetic fear. You have a feeling that someone is examining and observing. If you have been in their space crafts, you can remember all that during hypnosis. The evil ones usually do not come into your homes, they usually take telepathy and send it. The Others can come into your homes and show themselves. Provided that the evil ones come into your homes, it would be best to leave for a while and when you come back you purify your home and yourselves.

You can practice meditation through your body by repeating Amen until you find the light within you.

Children of the Earth,

You will realize how short a human's life is. Very little time and a lot to do. You will realize in the grave when the Hawks are watching. This means the Hawks guard your sleep when you die. The Hawks of judgement, whose eyes penetrate everything that you are, and everything that you are not. When this time has come, you can no longer regret through your bodies or thoughts. You cannot do anything that you have embodied with your body or what you were willing to do. When the right time has come, you will have to account for everything that you have done and your hidden thoughts. You have to account for thoughts that you maybe never fulfilled. But there will be new opportunities to others who did not have red flowers in their grave, and you can only think of your bodies that you cannot have back.

When others come and get another opportunity to go back to Earth, maybe you do not want them to have that opportunity. Maybe you want them to never again survive a living life, you who no longer has a chance. This is how the evil enters the lives of those who are given another chance to make amends, they want to destroy this opportunity. When the evil has entered your life and you cannot get rid of it, you have to go searching for help. If this evil has come into your life materially, and they are a person in your life who has made your life unbearable, you have to overcome this evil. You cannot fall into its temptation. When you fallen into the seduction, you have to redeem this seduction. This means that you might fall in love with someone whose only purpose is to tempt and seduce you. When this happens, you will drift into evil that in the end wants you as its own, but when you come to regret this seduction, the flying saucers will come to help you. Men are here and we want to help the Children of the Earth, who live in the dark and who do not know what the light is.

When the light is, you will know what the light is.

When the darkness is, you will know what the darkness is.

When evil comes into a small child who does not know how to fight it with the angels, your work is to help the child. You will realize that a healthy child that cannot be content either inside or outside is in the power of evil. Humanoids will come and help, with fire and water you must purify the child. You have to take holy water and when you rock the child put holy water and the evil spirit will leave. You can put fire in a small container where it can burn. You begin this by putting holy water at the bottom and then oil on top of it, and then fire. Then, you begin to pray that Satan would come and take away his own, when you pray, "Our Father", you will see that the child will calm down and fall asleep. When you demand Satan to take his own away, the child will cry and scream and shake and after this, you will pray, "Our Father" again. When the child has been cleansed, you can pray every night for him so that the evil will not return. When you get reassurance that everything is over, you can begin to live in a regular way again. The evil will come to the child if the child has been dealing with evil in their past life. Usually, the child has been Satan's Child and he wants to claim the child as soon as the child has been born. When the child comes back to Earth, he has usually been given another chance, and for this reason the evil wants to destroy him as soon as possible.

When you find out that "someone" who is in this small child, is not the child, you get scared and want to make a promise where you do not want to keep this child any longer. Many have done this without realizing any reason for their own actions. They cannot understand that they want to give up this child who they do not love, they do not understand that they want to give up the child because there is an evil spirit in the child. When you realize what is really going on, then maybe you would like to keep the child to help him. When you do not want to keep a child that seems strange, then maybe you are evil and want to destroy the child. For some parents, their only mission is to destroy a child who has received a chance to become better. When you realize that you have never cared about what has happened to you, then maybe you will realize that it has happened so that you can choose Satan. Some have a difficult destiny, and they remain good and calm because they have this information, and they know it with their body. When you realize that many bad things have happened to you that could not have been prevented, then you might have been one of them who Satan is fighting to have as his own.

Humanoids come to humans so that you can realize what will happen. Men are a part of God's great family, and we want you to receive us as friends, not as enemies. Men come to bring our brothers, the Sons of the Earth a message. We want you to have light to what you do not realize and what you cannot understand. You want life to be fun and easy, and when life is fun and easy, you get bored. When you are not even ready for a fun and easy life, you have to learn things so that maybe one day, you will be ready for a fun and easy life. When we come, you cannot know when we fly over your cars, when we come into your dreams, or when we begin telepathy. Men come to you but not in the way you think. You can never know when we are here and when we are not.

Behind that is Satan, who says that although you want to waste your time to do good, you will just become worse. Provided that you are evil, then you cannot do anything good, everything that you do turns into evil. When you try to be good but events that follow are always bad, through this you will realize that you are evil. When you realize that you are evil, you no longer have to try to be better than what you are. You can be what you are and that is better than trying to pretend that you are good when however, you are evil. When you realize that you are evil and you do not know how to love, and neither do you want to love, and when everyone near you has become more evil, then you will know that you are evil. When you still want to believe that you are good, you will do good deeds and when they turn evil, you realize that you are evil and there is nothing you can do. Good people make good things happen, when they do things, they turn good no matter what they do. When they meet people, they want to become better humans. When they help others, those whom they have helped become better humans. When we explain that Satan himself says that it is not worth it to do good, we meant goodness that is truly good.

Men are here to explain what is happening on Earth.

Nobody can begin and end like Men, we come here so that we can give an explanation to those problems you have here on Earth. Men come and explain what is going on Earth, so that you can understand what it all is about.

We want you to know what is going on, and when you know, and still through your bodies you do not want to understand, you will burn in Hell. When we explained that Hell is, and we explained that Heaven is, and we explained that there is a place where the Hawks guard you, when you are waiting for your judgment. When you have done evil and you have to wait for each one you did evil to come. Then, you have to go to the underworld. When everyone is present, the judge comes, and you get what you deserve accordingly. The judges are men who you do not know. These are holy men who have written down your lives. When you go to the place of judgment, you meet those Men who you have met here. We come to the place where judgment waits for those who have killed, hit and caused a lot of suffering, we come and give judgment. This justice is only for those who do not understand what is good and evil is. For those who still think that they are good, and who thought that they had the right to do the evil that they caused, there is no way out, not even for those who do not want to face their victims who are one of our own.

When you meet those who are one of our own, you have to help them, and you have to respect them. Many do not want to realize that someone they know is one of our own. They are different and they usually know how to help others in a way nobody else can. For this reason, never leave those interesting thoughts that are from minds that you do not know. When you do not know who this is, whom when you are near makes you happy, with your bodies you know that he is different. Never be mean to him, nor do anything wrong to him. If he is one of Men, then you will have to go to the judgment where Men are the ones who preside. When it is time for judgment, you will have to realize all of the things you did not want to understand while you were alive. When you realize all of this in judgment, it will be too late. You will have to go through what you have done. You might have to go to Hell, or you might have to be born again to a body that will be difficult to live in. When you do not want to love, and you do not want to be responsible for your actions, you will go to a place where you realize that there is no escape. All of your thoughts, all of your actions, and each of your words are here in the space between the body and spirit, which is called the underworld. You may yell, scream, and rage for someone to come and get you, but there is no one left who can come and get you. You will have to wait for the judge to come, and it might be that he comes one hundred years from now.

One hundred years in the underworld is a long time, and life in the underworld is not any better. You may want to come back to life, but you will no longer have a body, and your thoughts that you are so keen of will no longer help you. You are only a spirit, and everything that you are is subject to the Four Fires. These almost fireless fires, of which you will be, are what you were. If you never thought of spiritual things, then you will be in pain that can no longer burn away because you did not do anything about it when you were alive. This pain comes from a plane where your spirit had to wait for you to begin your spiritual life. When you did not do that, the spirit only experienced pain because it could not participate in the development for which it came on Earth for.

When you have lived in the choices where you were always wrong, you will go to the judgment where Satan is himself. He wants to personally receive all his faithful assistants, and his thoughts for you are that you can never come back on Earth, but instead will assist him in the spirit world where you will be his slave like we have previously explained. Meeting Satan is never a fun time. He does not care about your time, he has his own time which will come full when it does. You cannot have any hope at this point, nor will you have any hope. When you do not care about what you do during your life, it is a waste to even think that you can do something about it after you have died.

Humanoids also want to explain about what happens to someone who did evil due to a difficult destiny. Their judgment are the Eagles we have mentioned above. These are the Eagles of destiny. They contact you during your sleep like we do, and they produce telepathy that helps you to understand your own destiny. Those who become evil because they had a bad destiny will get the Eagles as their judges. These serious men are spiritual beings who have never been alive. They see everything that happens in you. They seriously follow every thought that goes on in your head, they rule destinies. When you were not evil, but became evil because of your destiny, the eagles will give you a life where you can still reconcile. We do not wish to explain more about them anymore. The Eagles will begin a mission together with us and will help by making decisions so that destinies can change. Their mission is to control death and the living life, and in this way, they are your enemies.

When you realize that you were never what you were supposed to be, you will meet a spiritual being that the helpers will bring to you in the underworld. He is a specific spirit through whom the Storks will come and explain what happens to the Children of the Earth. This spirit is one of God's angels who will affect you in a way that you will realize what kind you were supposed to be. This angel is one of the ones who comes to help humans. He is bodiless and he has never been flesh. When you meet him, you will know what kind you were supposed to become and what you have never became. When you realize how far from him you are, then you will realize what you have done to your own spirit. This means that when you thought about what your origin was, you might never come back to that small family that you left from. This means that you might have had a home somewhere in Heaven, where all of those whom you know are. When you do not care about what your joys and desires are, and what you are, it means that you might never be able to go back there, where you once came from.

The Storks are not the only ones living at the top of the heavens. There are many different ones, some are evil, and some are good. There are many bodiless beings and many more. For this reason, you can never know who the one is who leaves when the time comes full. Anyone can be the one who takes you with them. God's Kingdom is so great that to be able to understand it, the human brain is not capable. When we explain things, we can only explain a small portion and from this subject we have only explained what was the easiest to understand.

The following was written to Lea from Men.

Begin with this:

When you wake up in the morning, choose a small positive thought and dedicate it to your new day. Think that today is a brand-new day that you haven't lived yet, and you don't know what it can offer. Think that maybe today you will learn something that is healthy and important, and maybe today you get to meet someone who wants to love you.

Although your days are long and boring, allow peace to step into your heart and allow love to fill your trust, and allow your thoughts to come and go. You are given a freedom to live each day again and a new opportunity to correct your mistakes and you can love and you can learn to love right. When you learn to help and forgive, then you have learned a lot.

When you have learned that there is life everywhere then you have also learned about love

The following are parts from direct verbal contacts.

It is not the time to reveal everything yet, overcome your fears, and be patient.

Adam:

You want to develop spiritually; it has a price. Light, you are here to learn from the darkness. This is your secret school, you are perplexed. From darkness you have to search for God, your light has been taken away, you search and you search… in a way this is your hell.

There are secrets, not all doors will be opened yet, we are that door. Maria, you have had many difficult lives, you want to help people. There are many ways of how to help people, but you have to choose which way. Mona, if nothing else learn how to see the beauty and the ugliness in everything, but a coward is nothing but a coward.

THE FIRST UNIVERSAL LAW: EACH ONE HAS THE RIGHT TO KNOW WHAT HAS HAPPENED TO THEM.

There is a spiritual rhythm by which everything works. Your development determines whether this episode is good or bad. There are many different episodes, some smaller, some greater. When this episode comes, it is an abbreviation of the person's reincarnations, the same things occur until they pass (The same things repeat themselves until you have learned what was necessary and that's when they leave because you have learned the lesson.) Lea is like a diamond, developed in high pressure from charcoal. Your spiritual development belongs to you, you should be concerned for your own development. Spiritual development is always first.

Psychics sees events that have already happened, they see it in the astral plane. These are finer layers. The laws regarding mediums are different than that of a psychic. A true psychic can sense a person's different levels. Spiritual gifts are always questionable. Lea has been tempted a lot; she is humble. If the evil comes, she handles it.

(Translator: We asked a question about whether Men are the so-called Nordic race of humanoids.)

Answer: Men are not that race. There are many kinds in space, but they come first to themselves, each one comes first to themselves.

(Translator: We asked about Lea's trance compared to Edgar Cayce in trance.)

Answer: There cannot be any comparison, everything works in a different way. Adam also has his own opinion about the subject. Individuality is greatness. Absolute perfection, God's Greatness. God created man to perfect God. What you do to each other, is what you do to God. There are a thousand ways to say the same thing, and one of these ways leads to a path for one person. One sentence is a thousand paths to home, but there is only one home.

The human's first mission is to know themselves. As long as you are humans, be human, learn to live as humans, die as humans. This time that you are humans, could be your last, to be given a chance to learn is mercy. Many go to school to learn, nevertheless something within them remains unlearned.

The seed is within each human. Many wish to become rich, many have an empty soul.

Many want to be holy, they stop everything yet they are still not holy, within them there is a seed to be holy - an idea of God. When you are alive you are alive, when you die you have more. There is a seed of the knowledge that after death you have more. Life is a compromise of spiritual development. This spiritual development cannot be achieved without life. Only a living human in a living world can participate in this battle.

NEVER UNDERESTIMATE LIFE. The objective of the so-called love between a man and a woman is always higher learning, this is a secret. A human can receive information that can go away but when the awareness expands the information will remain forever. Sometimes the past is the future.

Adam:

Hold on to your rights, the evil wants power, the evil will withdraw in front of your rights. An evil person has no rights, study people who do not have the rights to themselves. You have a right, hold on to that right! This is not a play school! Adam tries to help us, and we have to help ourselves. Your wrong choices are Adam's wrong choices. Difference is of God. There is no difference in satanism, when you have met one then you have met them all. In divinity there is difference, each one is under their own laws. Many begin a hundred times from the beginning and end back in hell, they try and try and each time they have a drop more of Satan.

Spiritual development is cruel. You either speak on behalf of spiritual development or not. If you know everything about your development, it will not go as it should. UNIVERSAL LAW: Nobody has to love anyone they do not love. From lies you get bad karma, dishonest karma, you are here to learn what love then really is. It is God's love to teach, neglect is that you do not care. "The one who God loves, He punishes."

Divine truth:

Satan will always bow to God.

Satan will never bow to his own.

Learn how to be happy, it is not so difficult.

You have to always live for the future, also for the future after death.

Adam:

What happens fast? Death comes fast, birth comes fast, be ready! Fear is a great weakness, you have to be able to rise into your spirit.

THE FIRST LAW FOR MEN:

NEVER INTERFERE WITH GOD'S GREAT PLAN. THE GREATEST SIN, THE BIGGEST PRICE.

You do not have the strength to pay the karma.

Yes, God takes care of his own, yes God will avenge to whom avenge belongs.

Adam:

The secret of Atlantis:

Atlantis was ruled by high spiritual power, the spirit ruled the matter, the spirit was conscious. Of course before Atlantis there was the so-called Paradise where God's created human existed. Paradise humans built Atlantis. Satan withdrew with his troops elsewhere, he was one of the Atlanteans. His only mission was to destroy Atlantis and it happened because it had to happen. Men were Atlantean. People want to know about God but not Satan. Atlantis is somewhere else; it is your choice where you go. An angel versus an evil spirit. Do not be afraid of evil, if you were afraid of evil you would not be here. Search for the spirit! Habit is not trust. God is easier to reach in church. God does not give you pain, you lack happiness. Learn to know yourselves. If a sudden feeling comes: hate, love ...etc. is it a feeling from the spirit world?

Search for the light.

Peace, God's peace, God's Great deep peace.

Try to eliminate fear.

Try to allow faith to grow in you, when you have a doubt, study it, when you have certainty then you have certainty.

If you doubt your value, then you doubt God.

Be worthy of your image: no judgment, no accusations.

It is never too late, everything comes by redemption.

Enjoy! Live!

You are given happy days.

You search only for spiritual development, a spiritual goal.

You cannot be weak.

You cannot follow anyone other than God.

You cannot look for saints from the Earth, humans need saints, Sons of God do not. We only need the truth.

If you want to develop in spirit you must rise above the human, you must be like a path.

You, yourselves have set the requirements.

You have to expand your consciousness. You need time, get used to God, get used to life, it happens slowly through slight nausea.

Build happiness into your lives, pray and study yourselves.

Prayer and meditation are the only strength in life.

Search for balance in your daily lives.

Spirituality comes first, then your higher self, then your intelligence, and then your feelings.

Fear prevents people from doing things.

Overcome fear, fear is a great weakness.

The answer can be found for everything, but you are not always ready to receive it.

Pray, be careful, be awake.

Adam.

Verbal connection:

Our ship is close by. Evil UFOs are nearby, that is where the bad vibrations are from. You have to learn how to have a calm and peaceful outlook on life. It is not right to think that you had made a mistake and you did wrong. Whatever had happened has already happened. You have to have the kind of attitude that you are ready to pay for your actions, if you have bad karma then you have bad karma. Fear disrupts spiritual development, you must have courage.

You have to have the type of life attitude in which whatever you have done, you are ready to pay for your mistakes. Take responsibility over your own actions and thoughts, if you want to develop, you want to see your mistakes and not be afraid.

What prevents animals and humans from getting to know each other? Fear. Calm your mind, accept everything that comes into your life. If you get bad karma, be ready to pay for it. If you make a mistake, be willing to learn from it. Look freely to the past and to the future. People are tested according to their weaknesses. Know your path and you will know how to walk.

The lion is a symbol:

It creeps quietly in the jungle and attacks, one can never know if it is attacking from the front or from the back. (Lion as a symbol of temptation it can be a personal weakness from the past, a wrong choice, or a weakness in the future)

Accept that you are one, yet you are never alone. Accept the truth. The more you escape loneliness, the lonelier you become. The better you accept loneliness, the less lonely you are. If you live for your body, then what happens to the spirit? If you live for the spirit, then what happens to the body? The body is the home of the spirit. If the body leads the spirit, the spirit dies with the body. If the spirit leads the body, the body can live happily one life. There is no reason for life to be easy. Life is not easy for anyone. You are here for your own spiritual development, save yourselves and by saving yourselves you can save others. You came here alone, do not imagine that you came here together. You cannot be together. You were not meant to meet God together. You live together, but that is not the purpose. Do not lose yourselves, be awake. You feel that it would be easier to be two than to be one. When you are one, then you want to be one before you become two.

Pity those who do not have the strength to love.

Love with justice, see that if you can, you give justice.

Do not search justice for yourselves because that does not exist.

Do not seek love for yourselves, because it does not exist, but instead seek love for those who are near you.

The Path of the Four Fires

Be a path for those without a path.

Be a door for those without a door.

Be voice for those without any one to listen.

All seeds fall into the Earth, some sprout, some die,

but all seeds fall into the Earth.

Not one martyr's tears fall into dry ground.

No one suffers purposelessness, not even the most innocent.

Suffering is fire that burns.

The evil has its time, but the time of the victims is never over and those who wait the longest will receive the most.

Pity those whose time is over because they will not be there, where their victims time begins.

Believe in strength because strength exists!

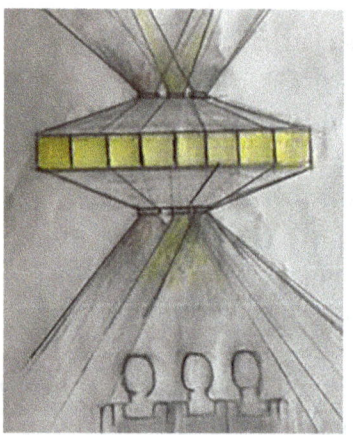

The above drawing was made from my memory based on a channeled drawing we received after we asked how the ship looked like. I remember the colors above and below are red, green, and yellow, but I don't remember the order they were in. The ship was silver with yellow windows and Men were bold, and tall and wore gray overalls.

We will never leave you, Children of the Earth, we always come back to help you.

How could we leave you, when the spirit that God gave you is the same spirit that resides in us.

Men will never leave you, but we will aways come back when the time has come full.

The profits of this book are intended to be used to bring this message to wider audiences and aid in humanitarian organizations.

Those who cannot afford to buy this book can request a free copy through our website www.thepathofthefourfires.com.

"There are many ways to love but only one way is right."

Men/Sons of God

www.ingramcontent.com/pod-product-compliance
Lightning Source LLC
Chambersburg PA
CBHW070532090426
42735CB00013B/2955